AF352447

FLOOD
EDITIONS

CHICAGO

BRIAN CALVIN

DAYS

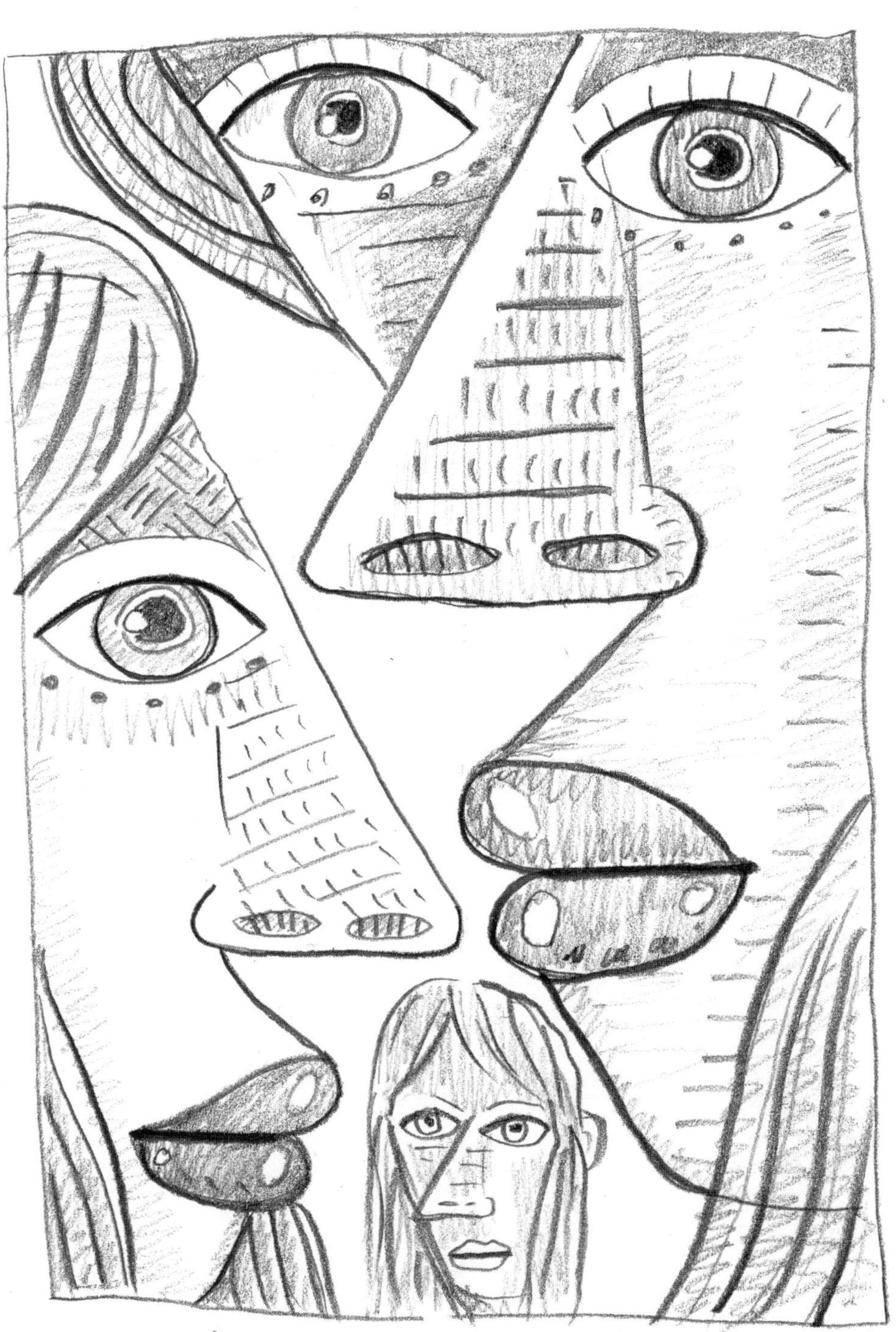

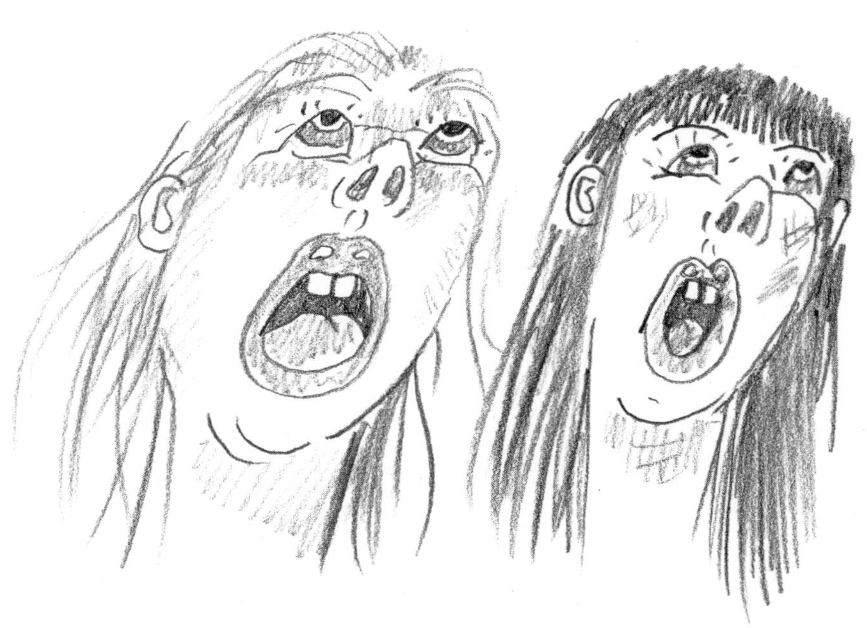

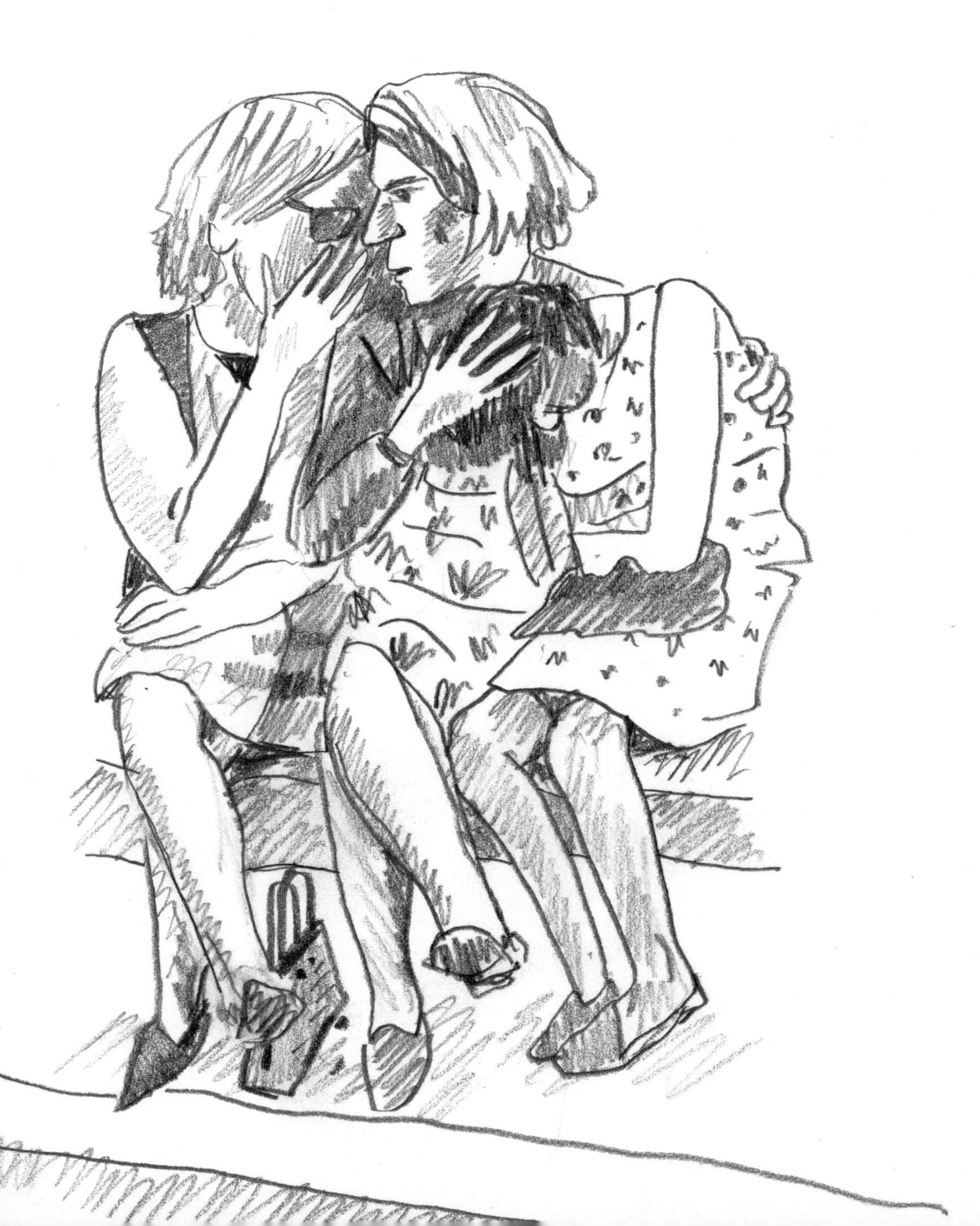

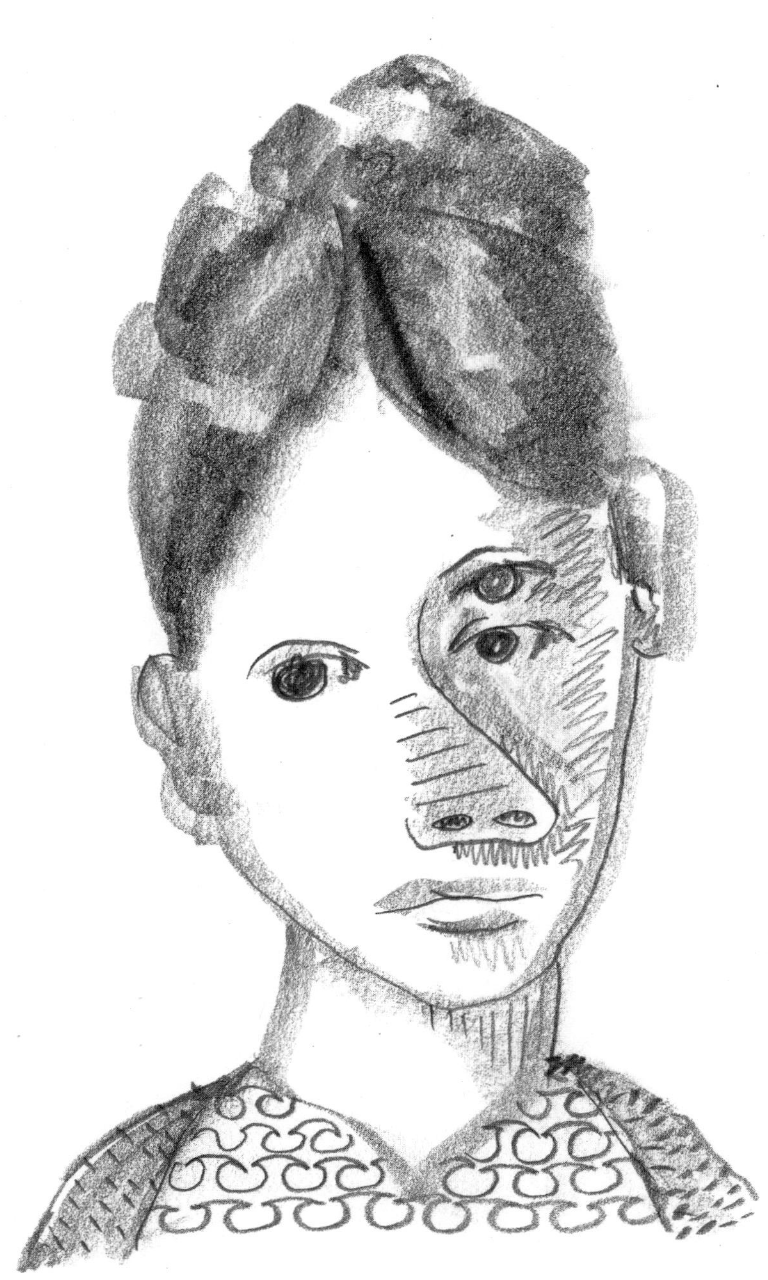

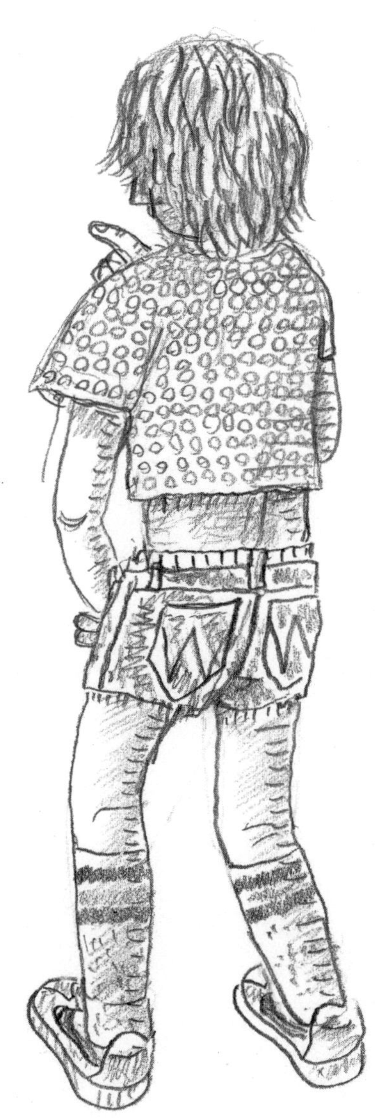

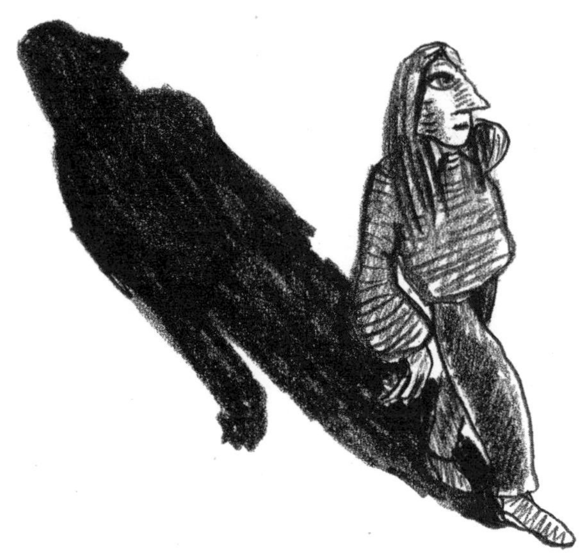

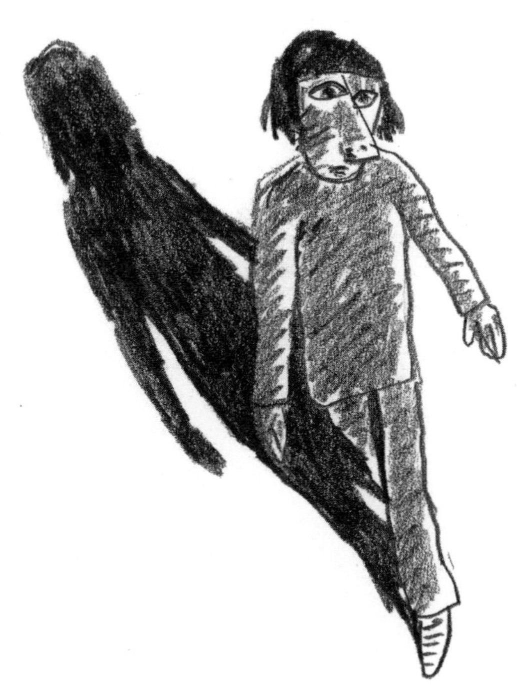

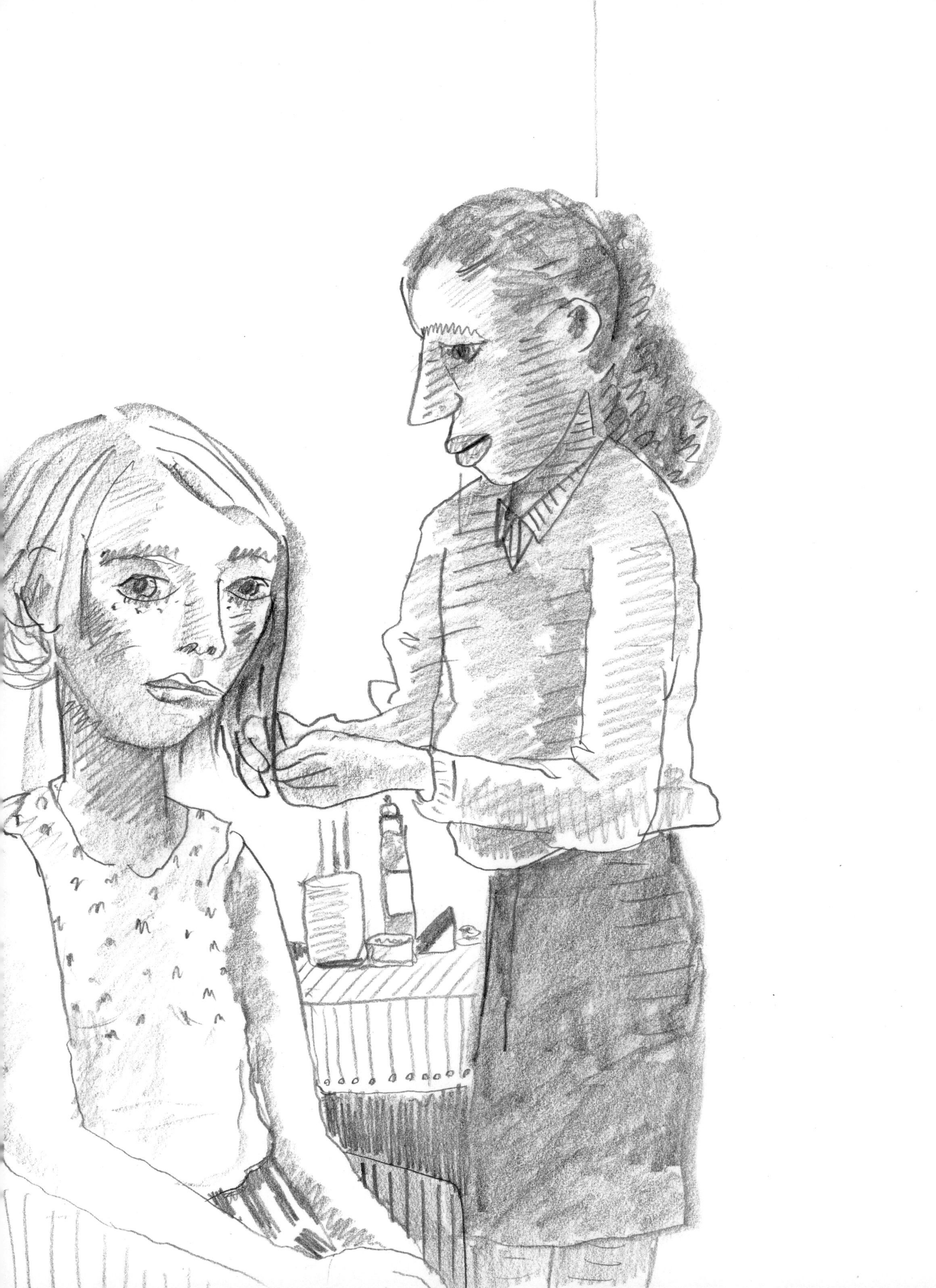

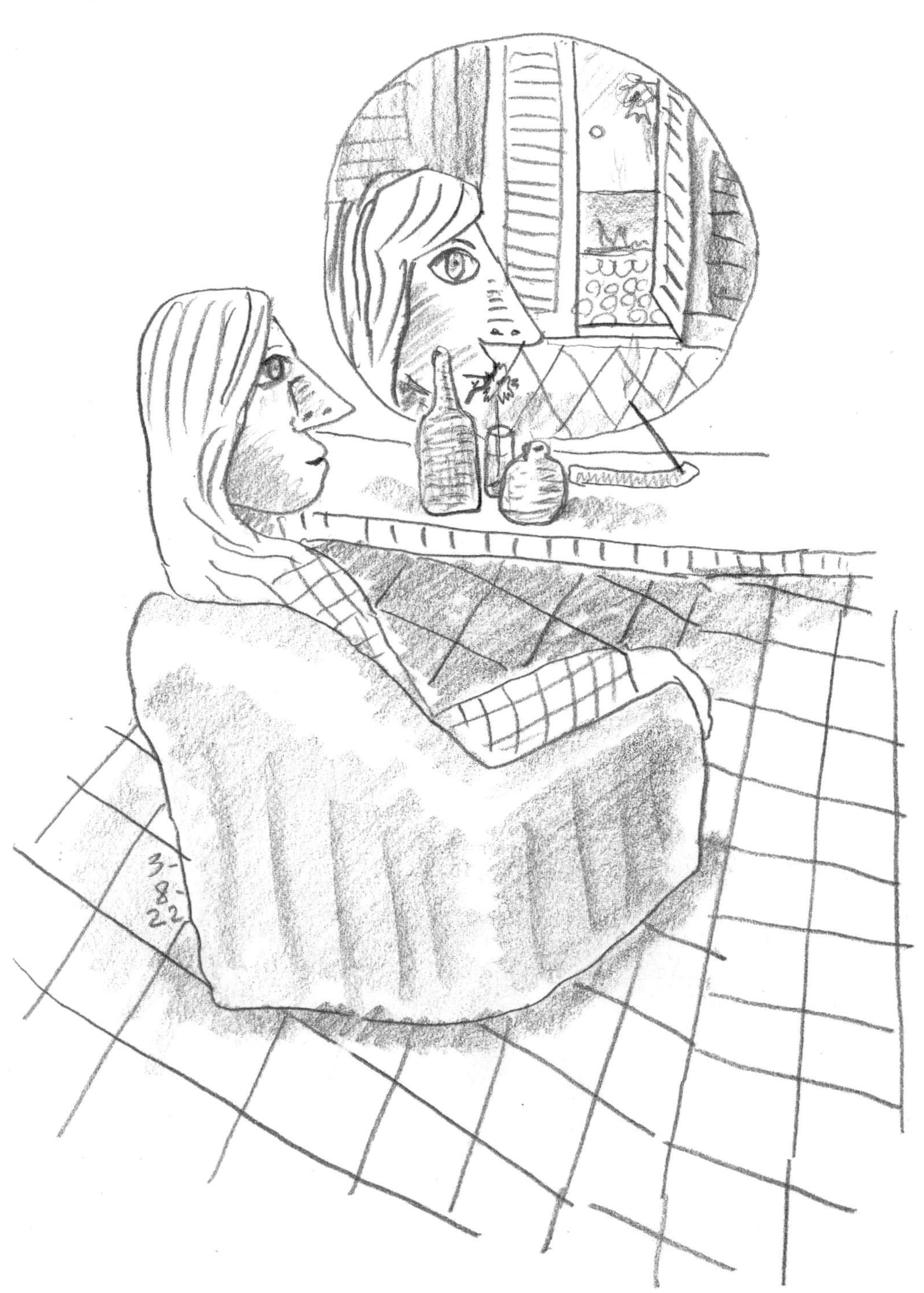
3/
8/
22

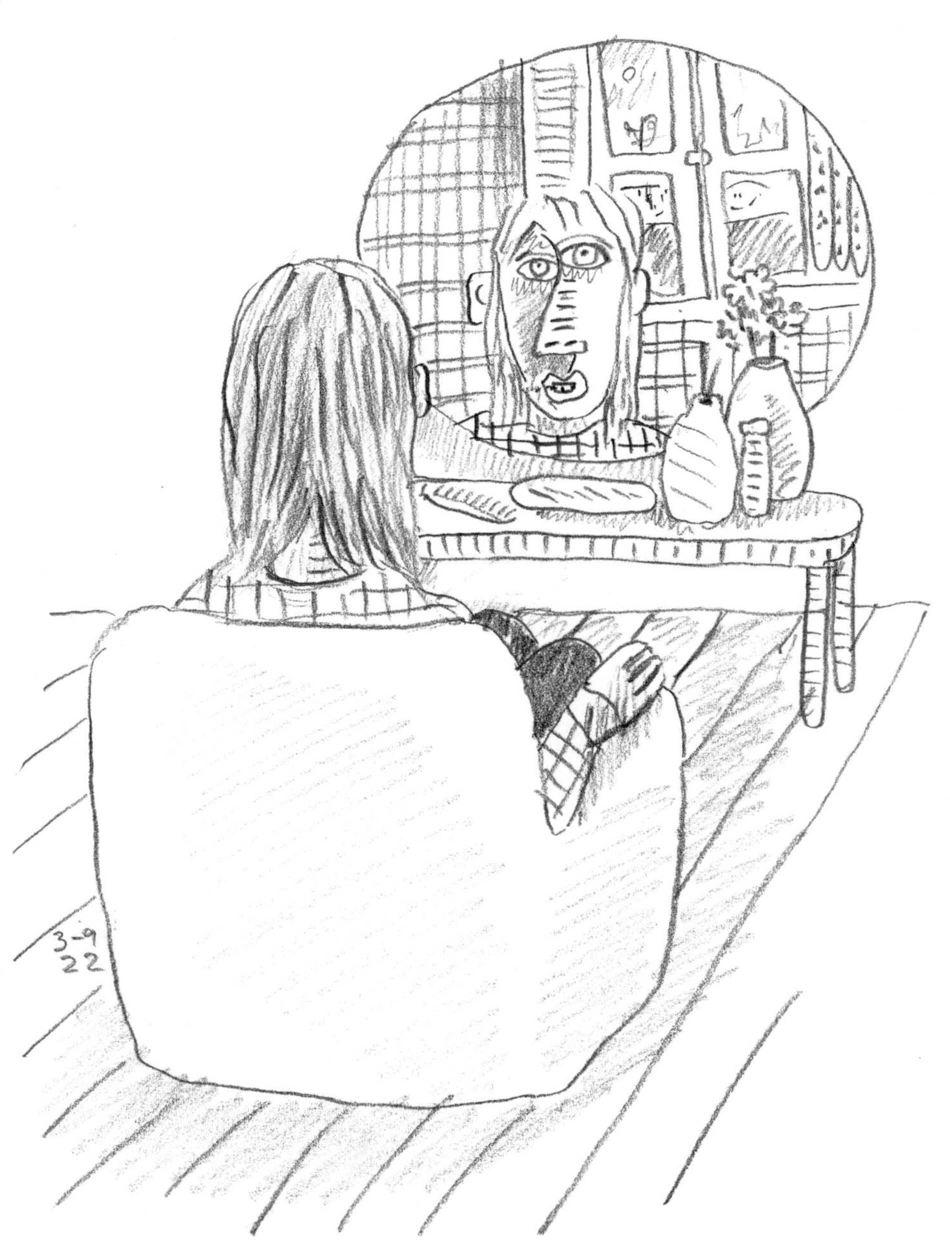

3-9
22

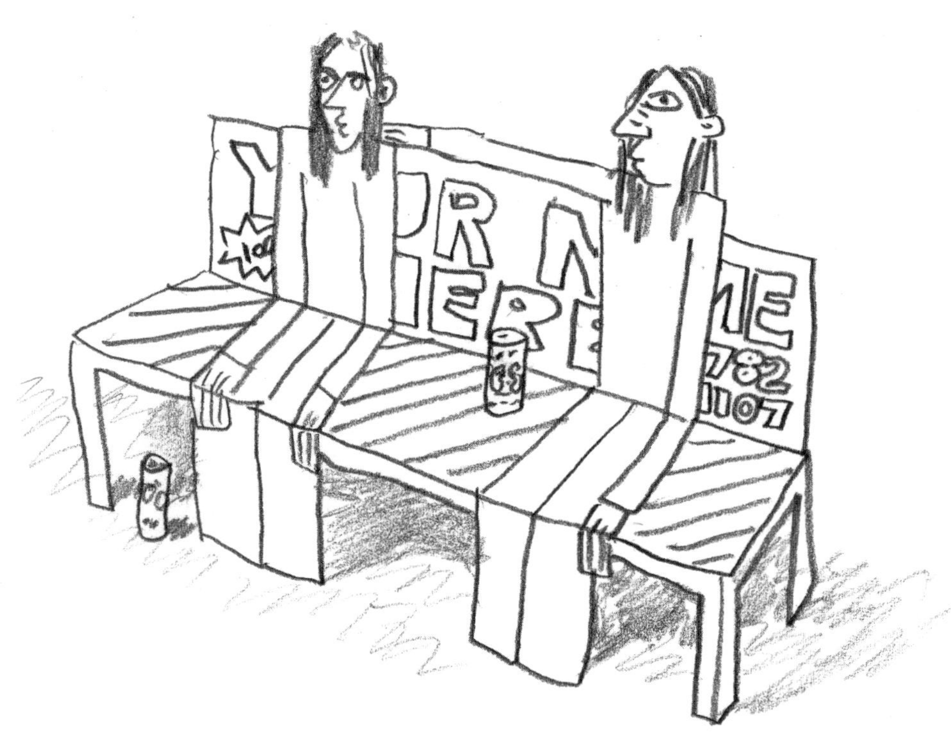

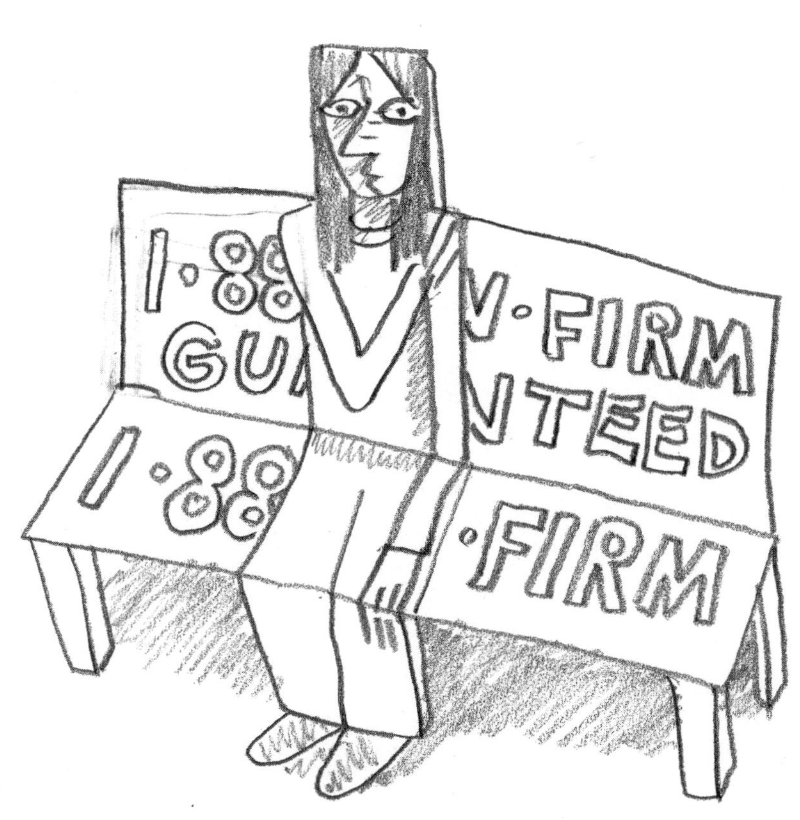

1·88
GU
1·88
V·FIRM
NTEED
·FIRM
FIRM

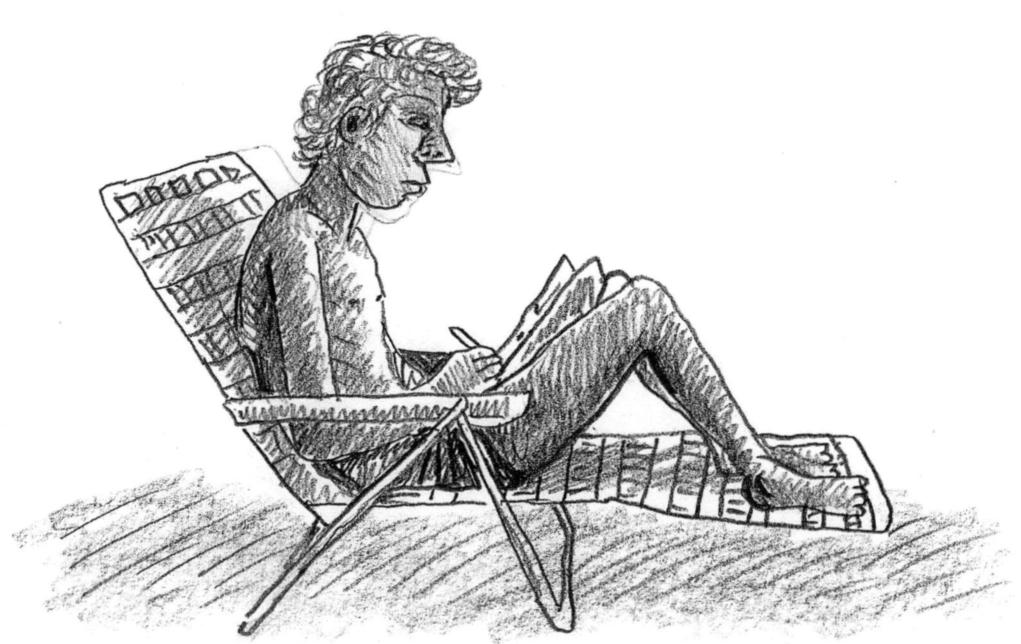

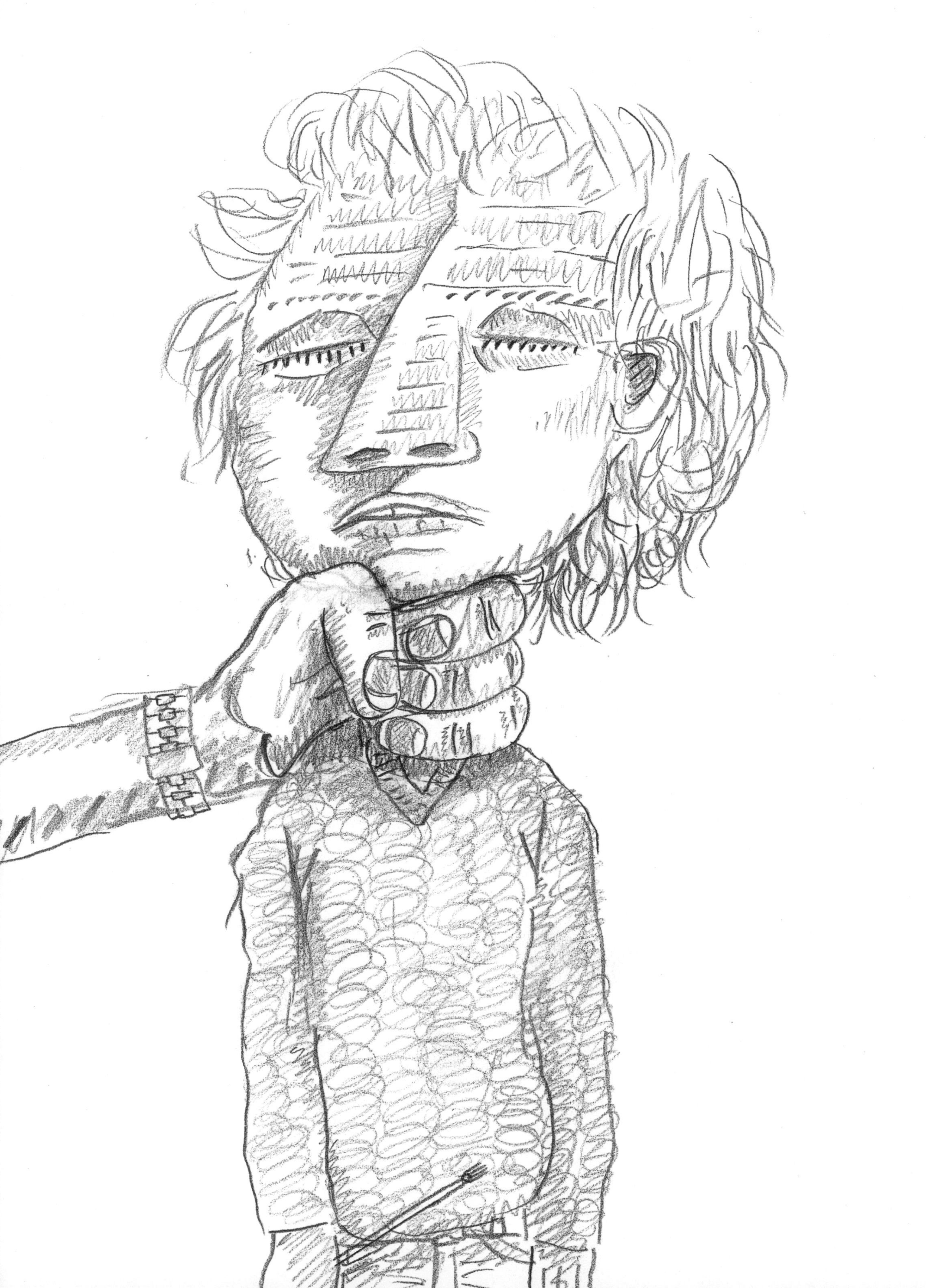

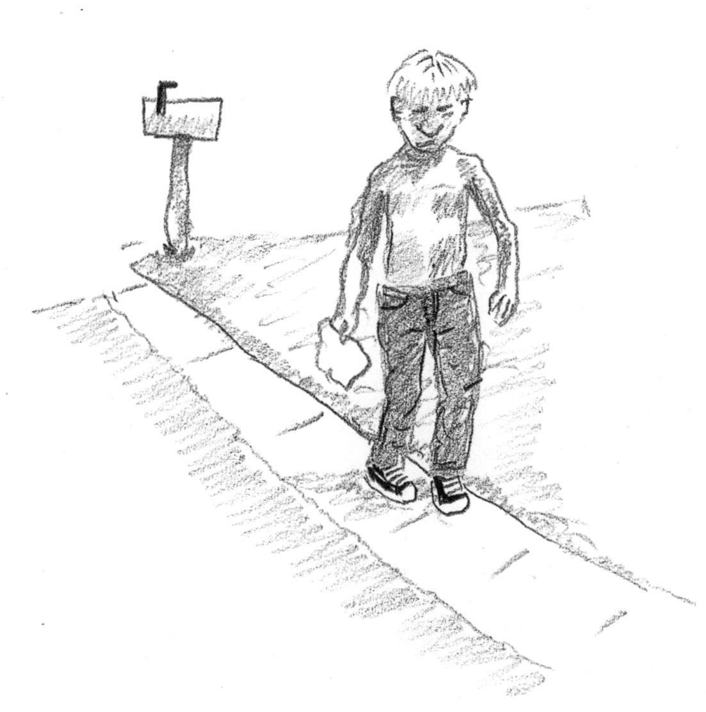

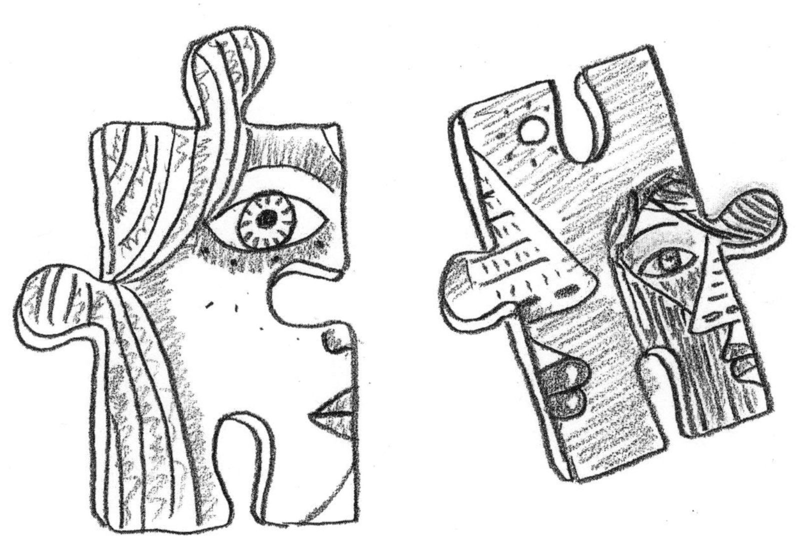

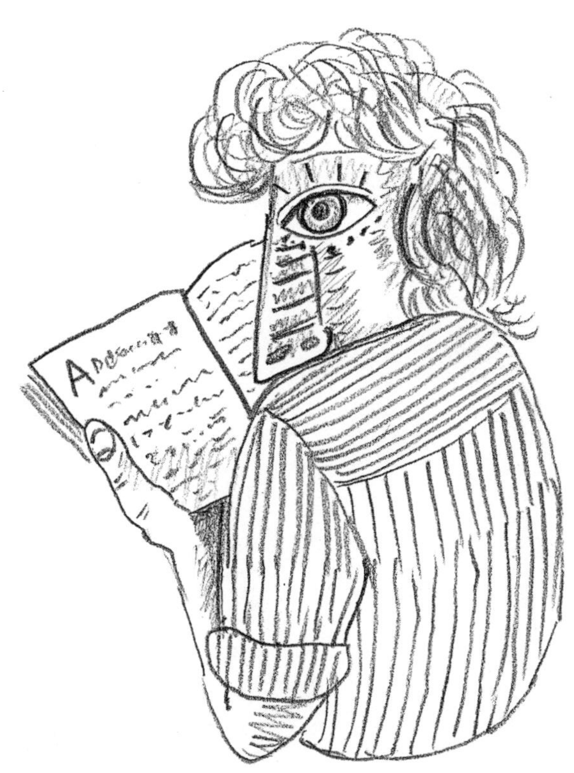

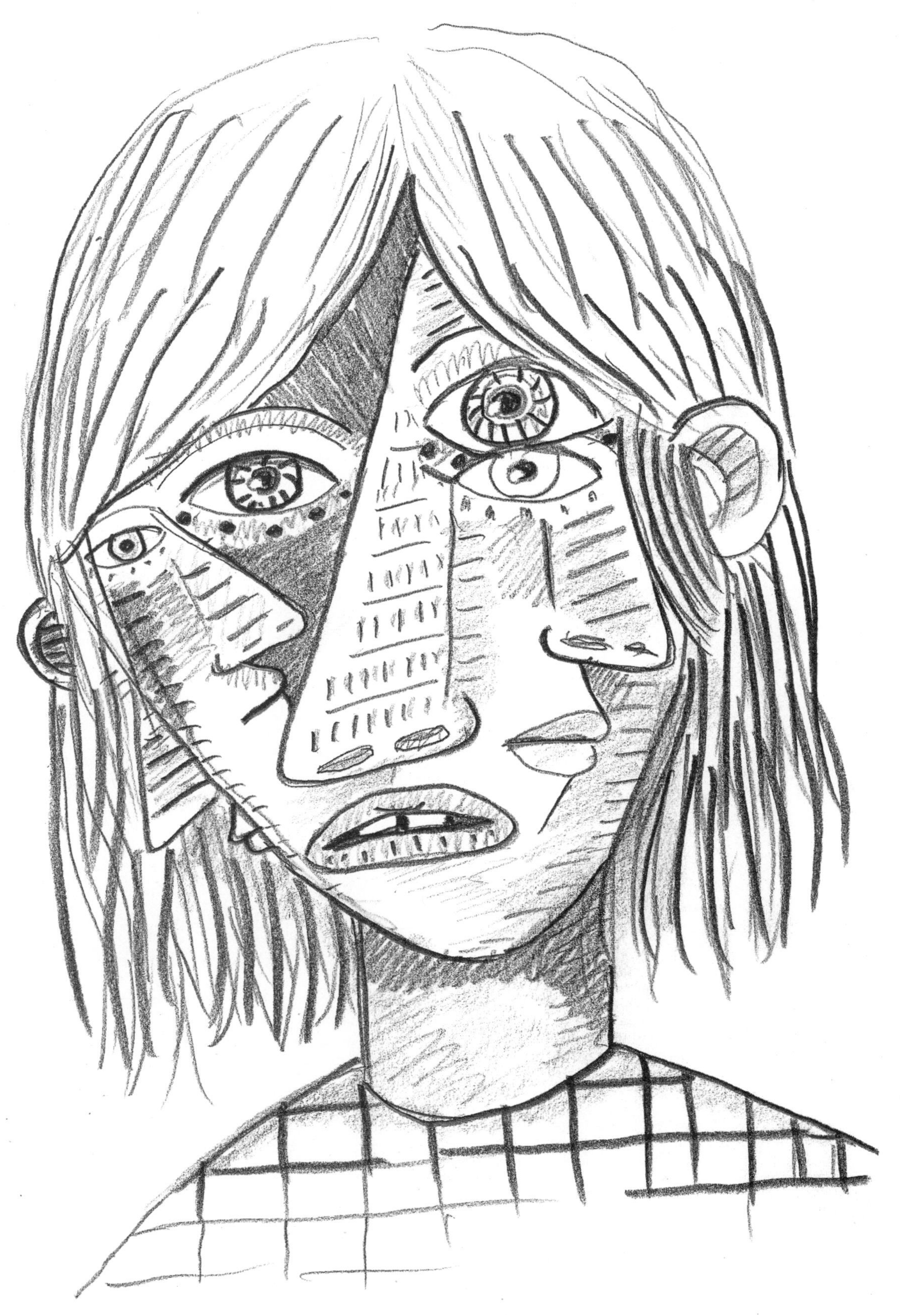

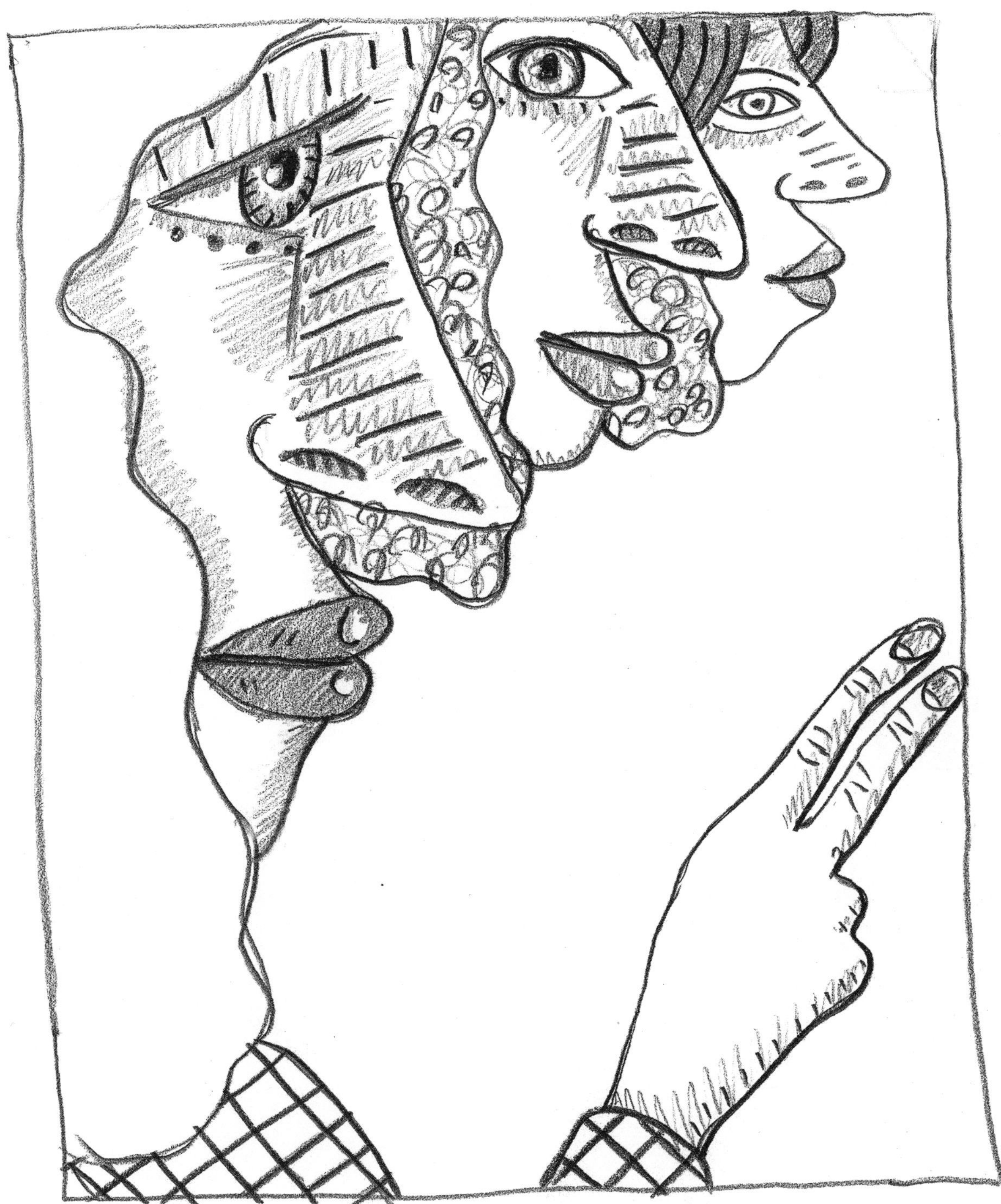

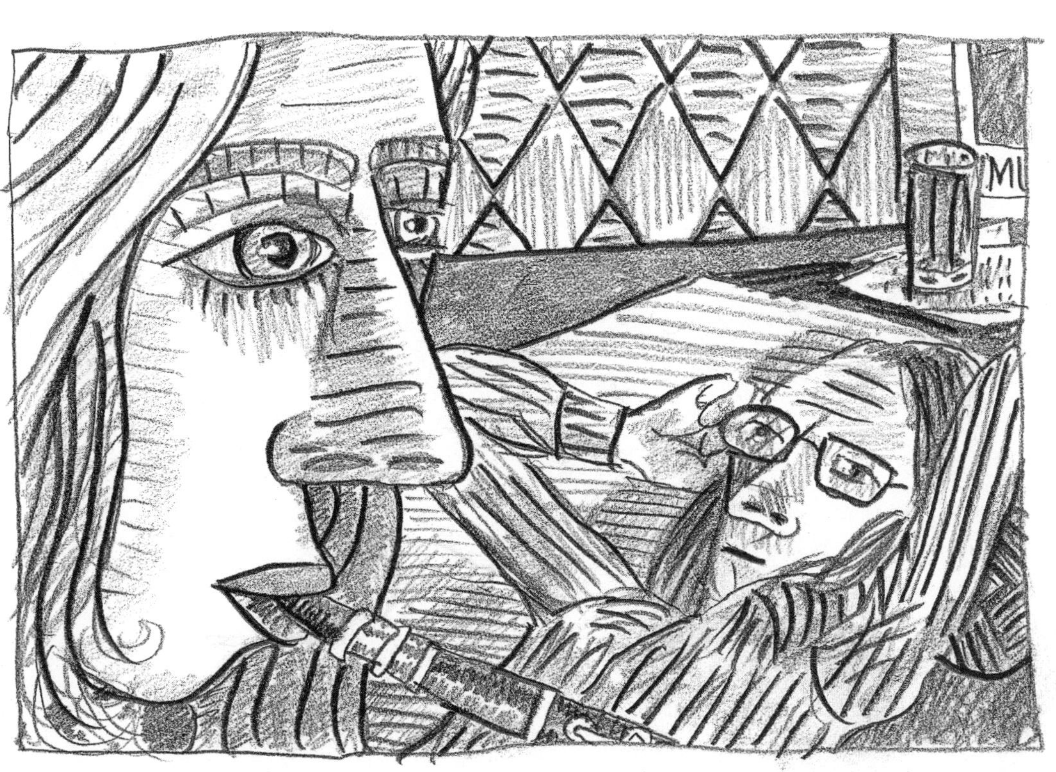

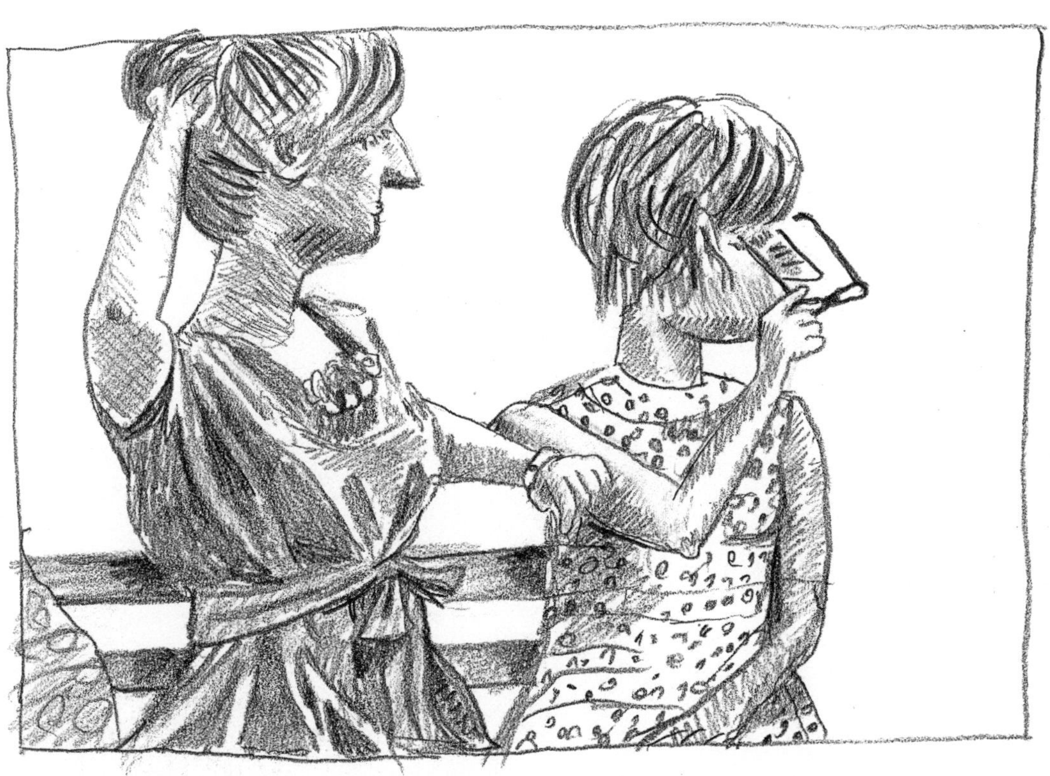

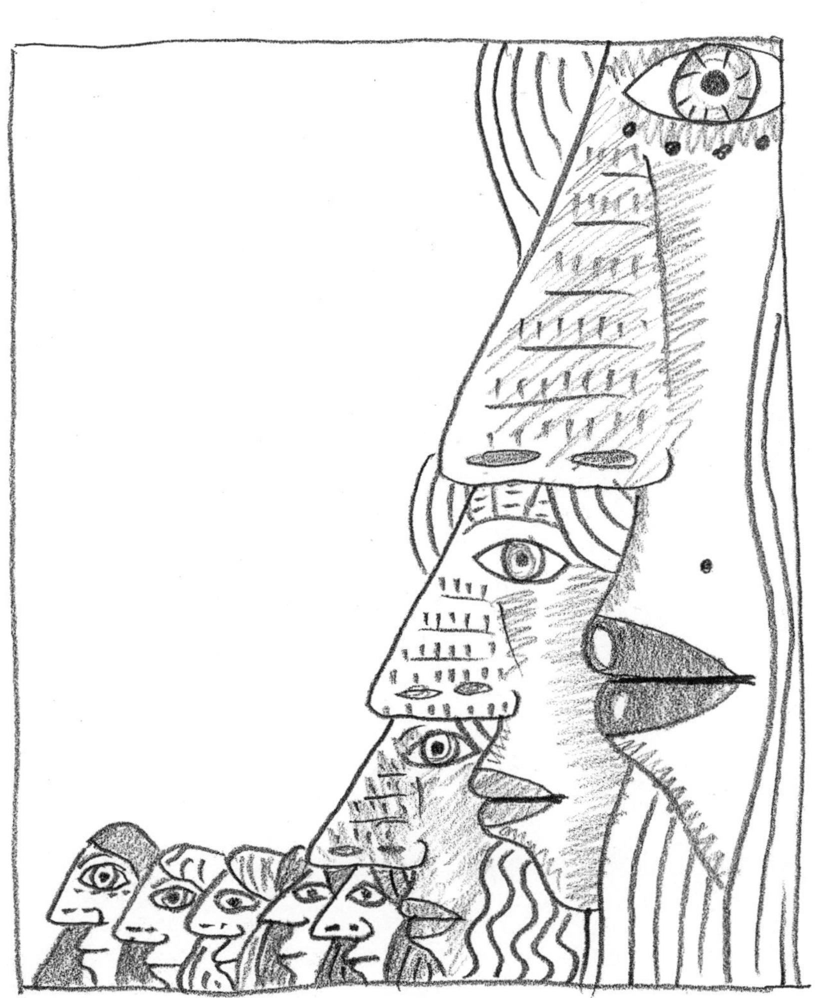

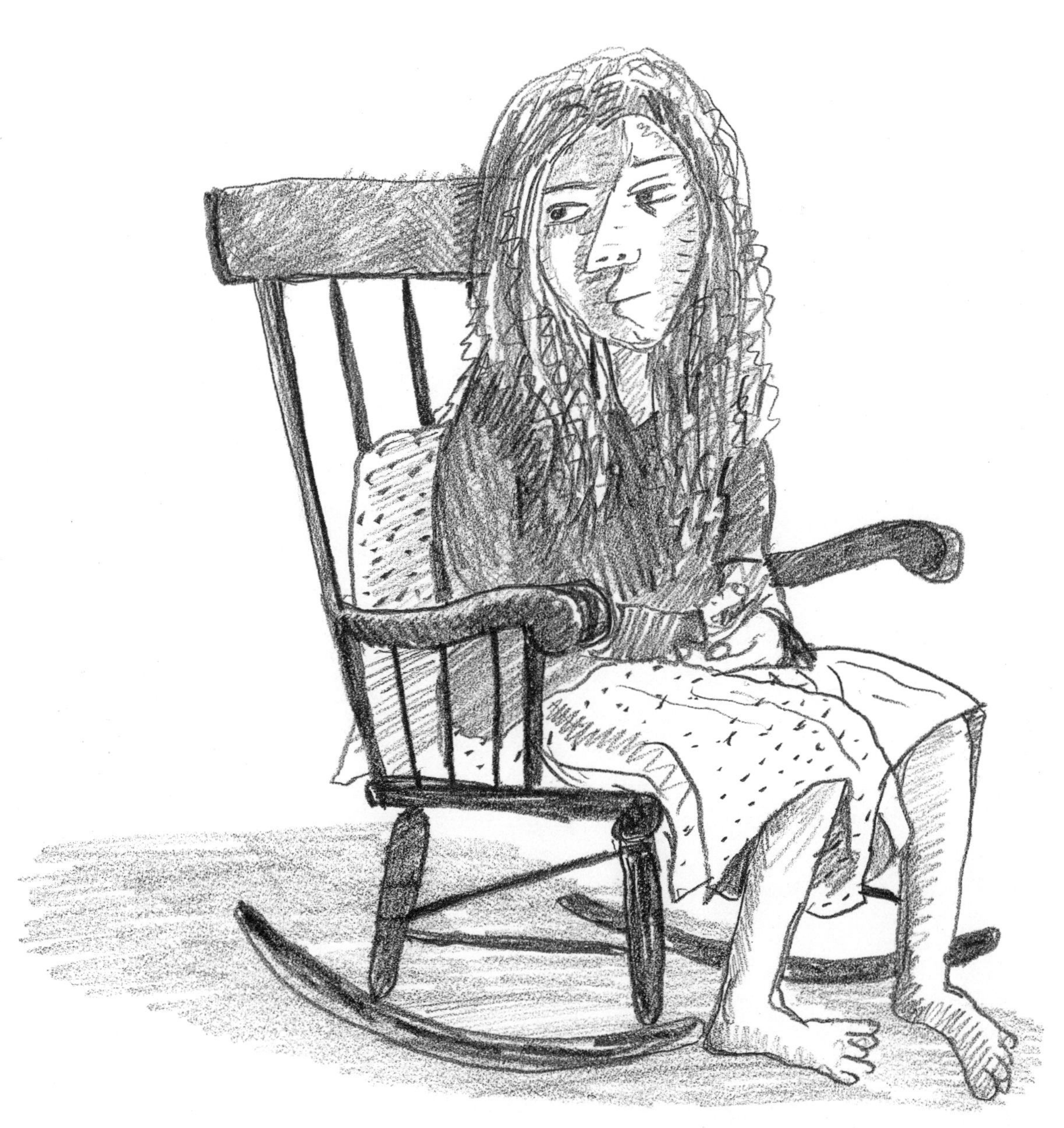

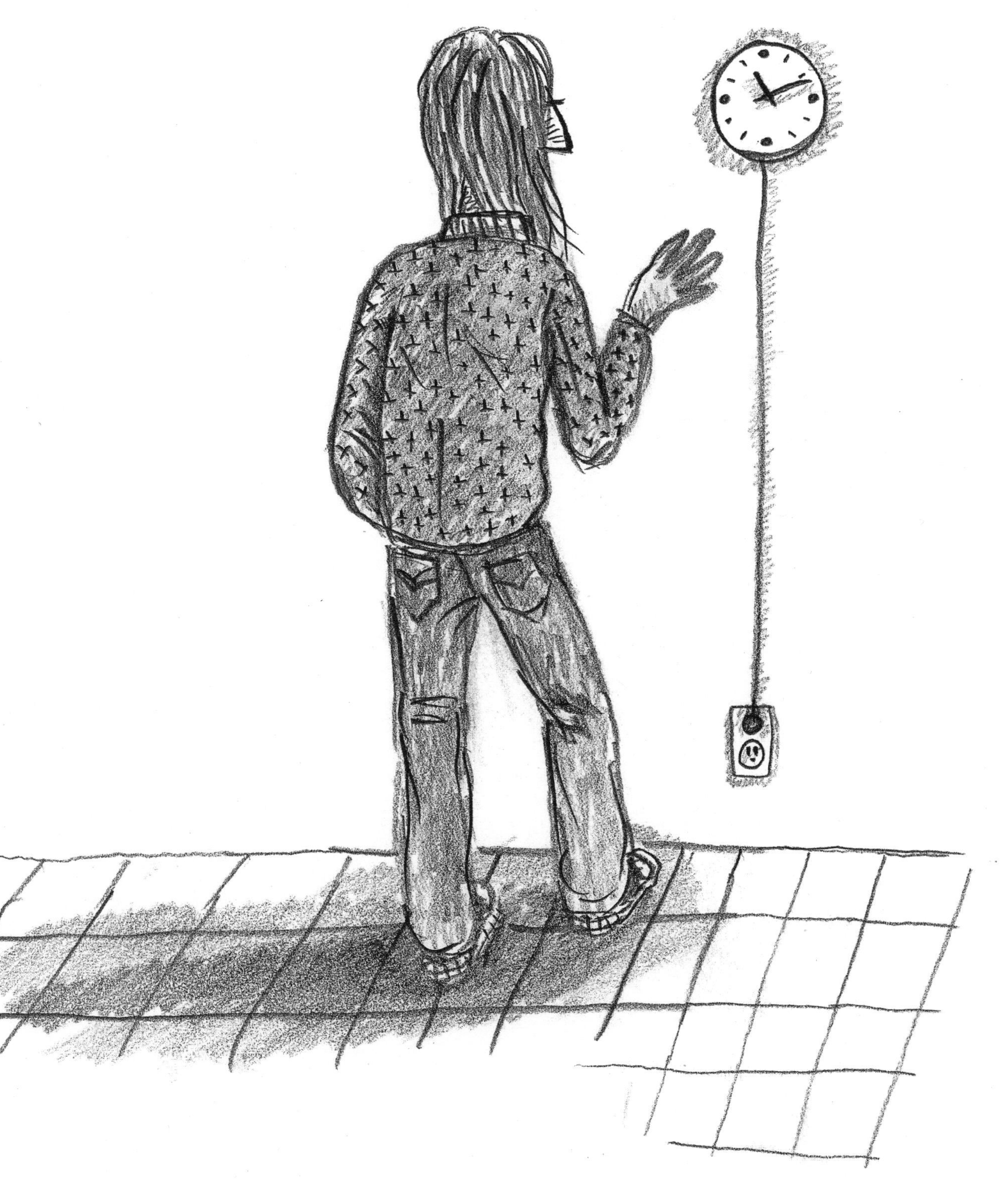

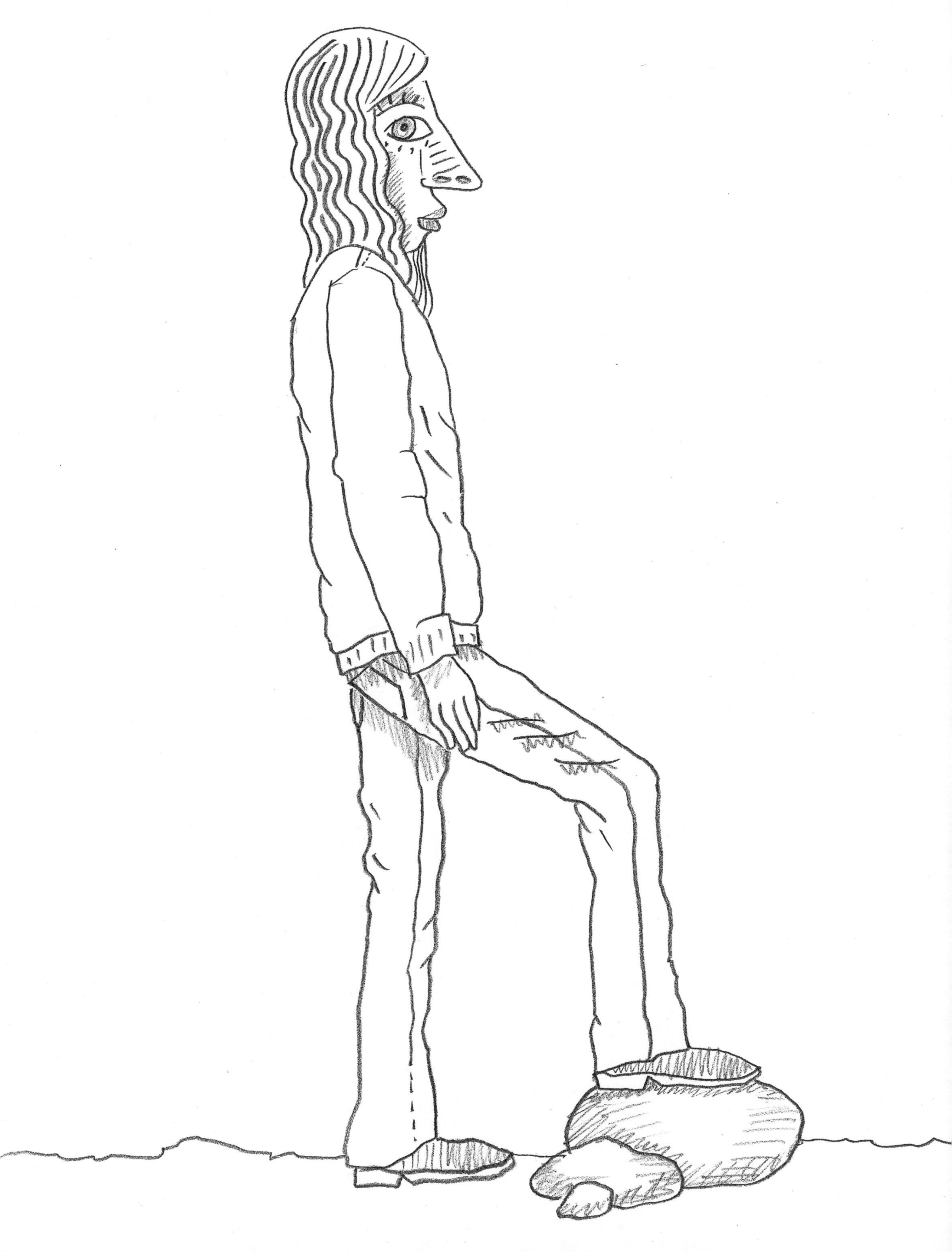

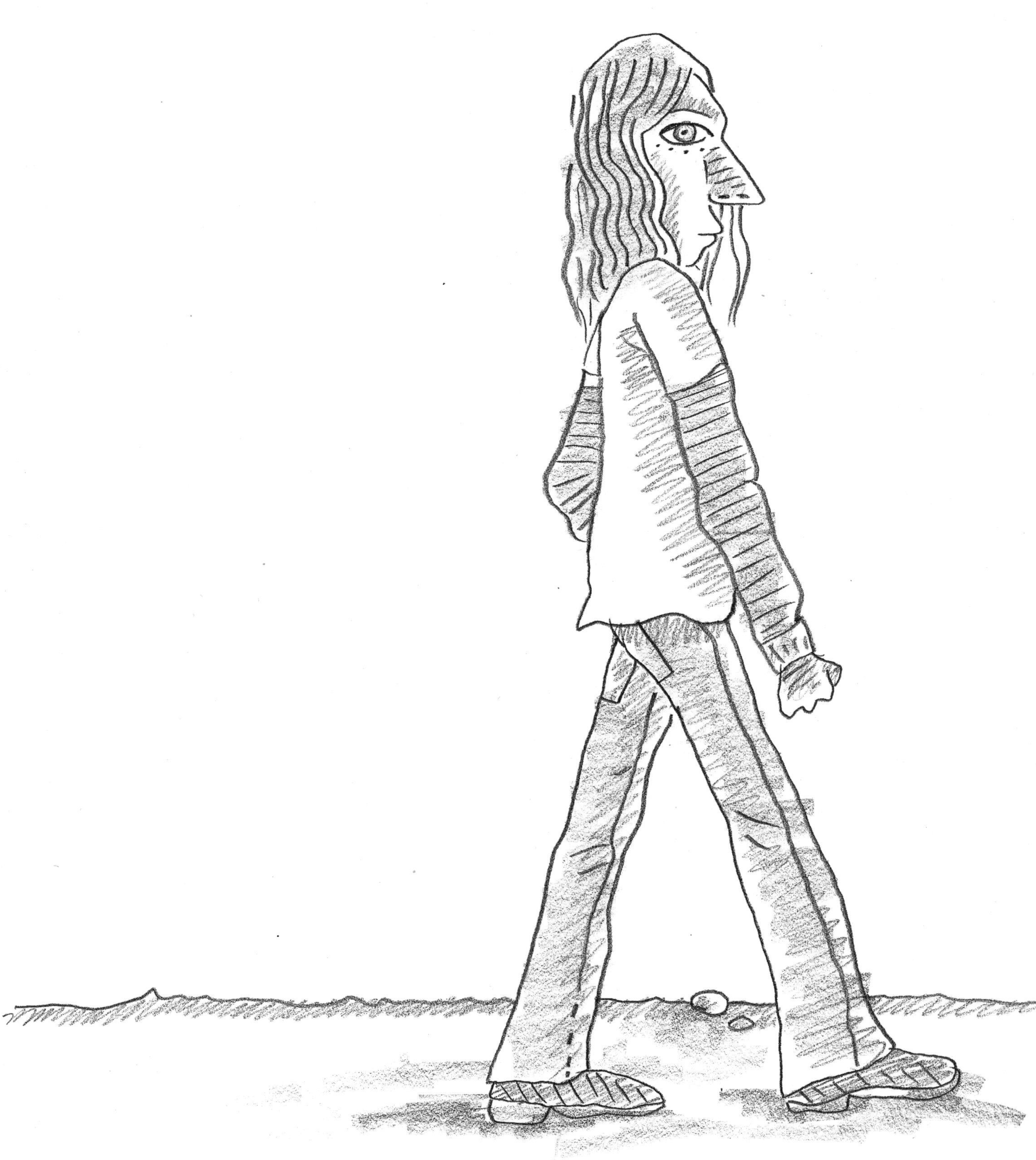

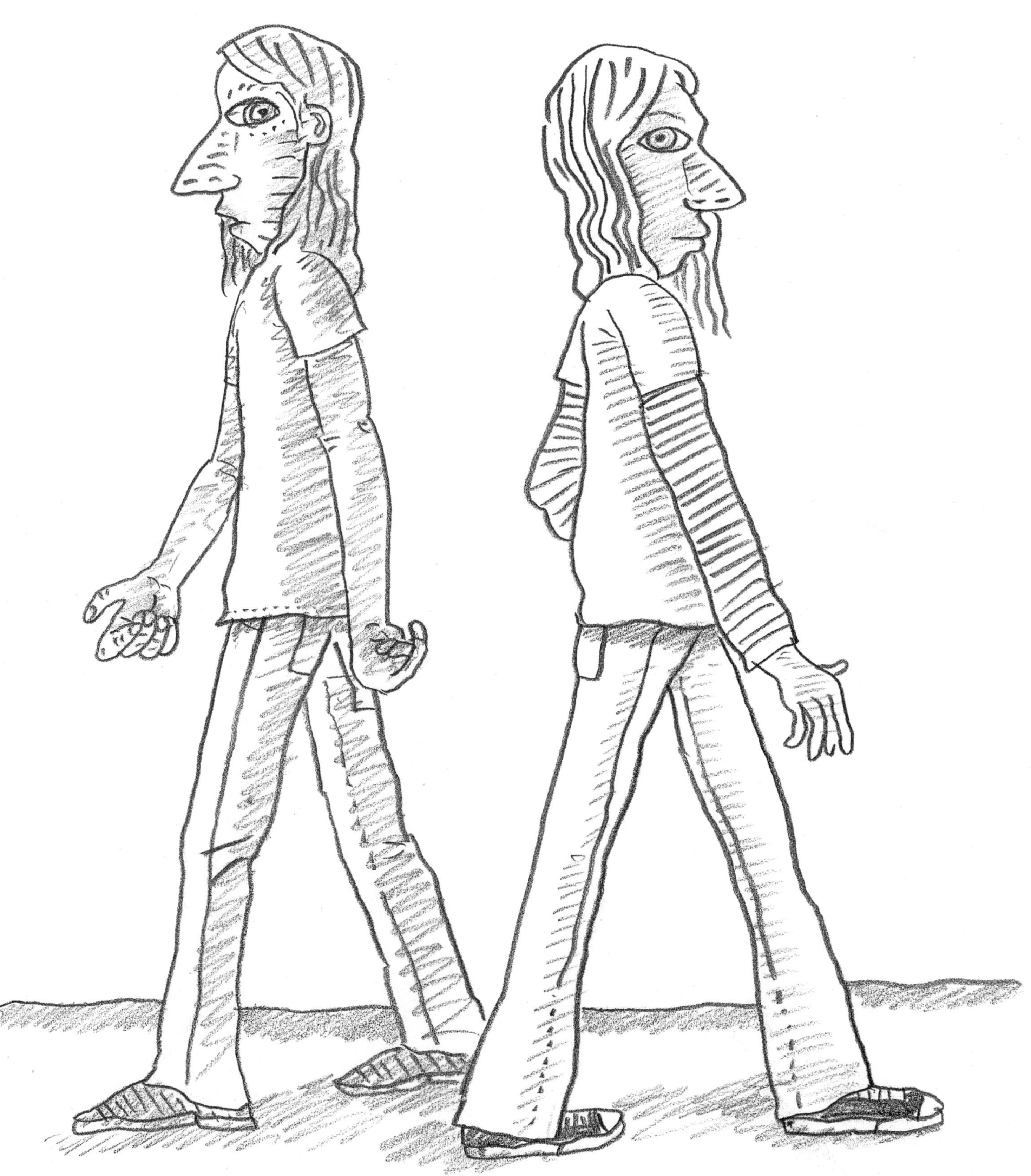

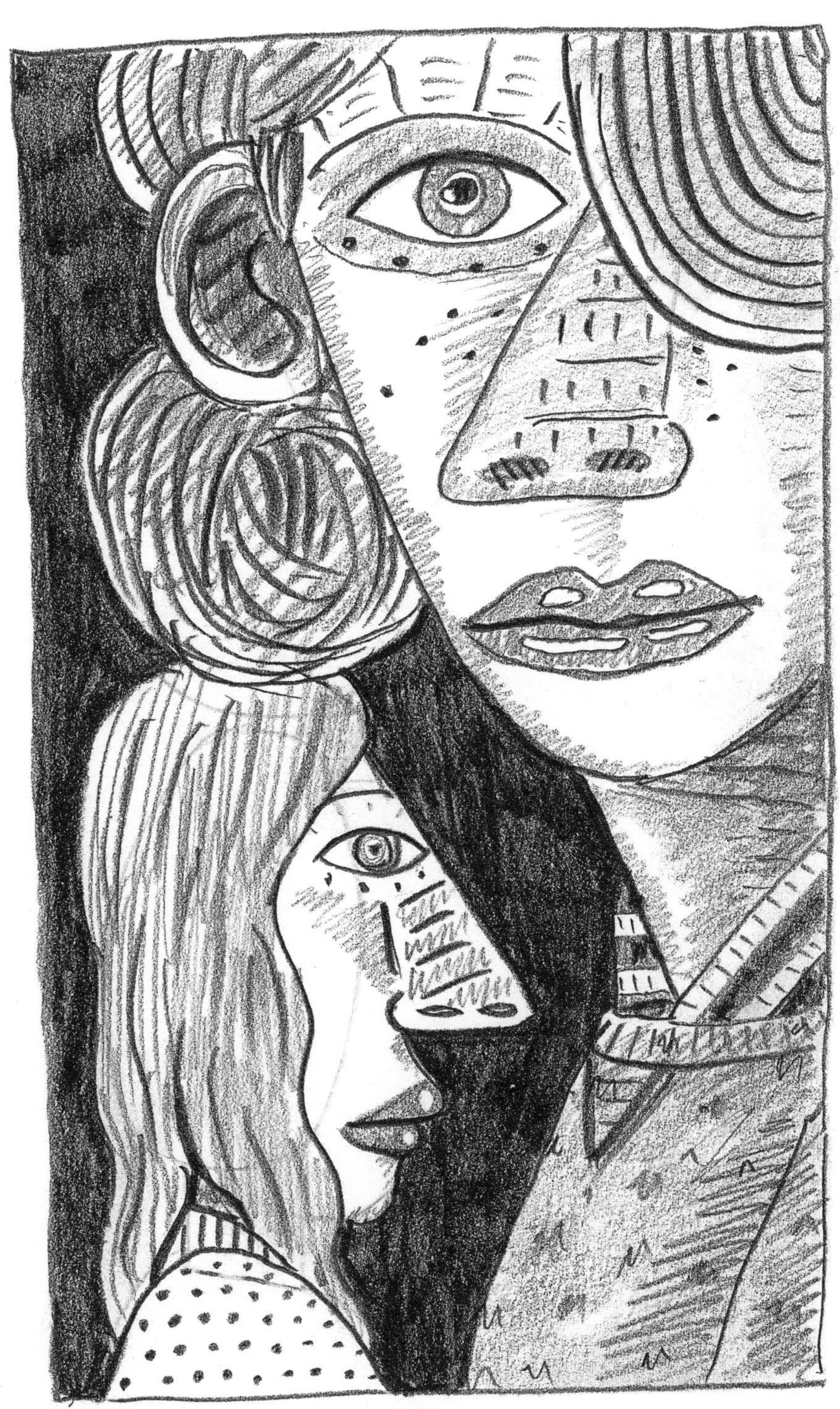

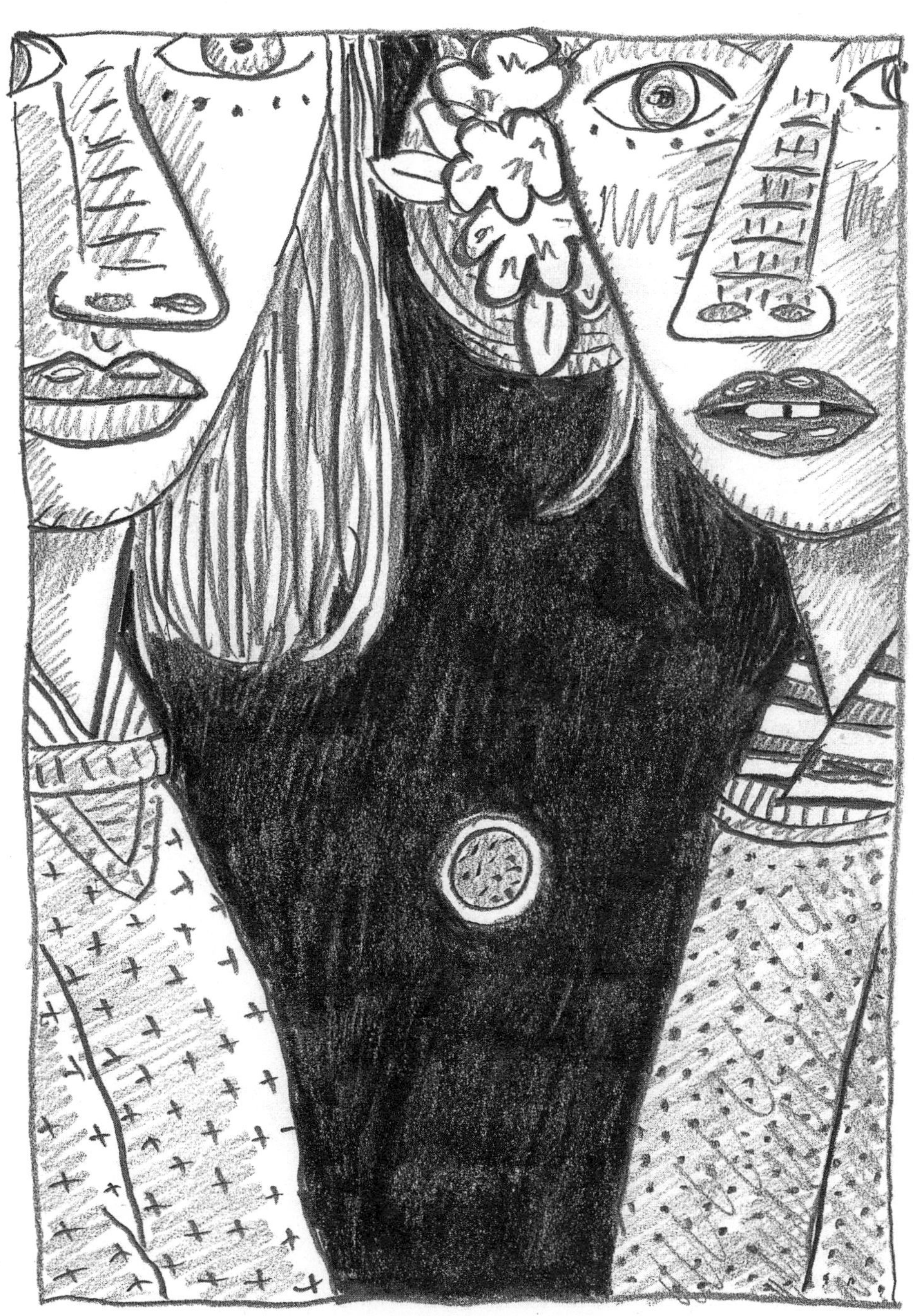

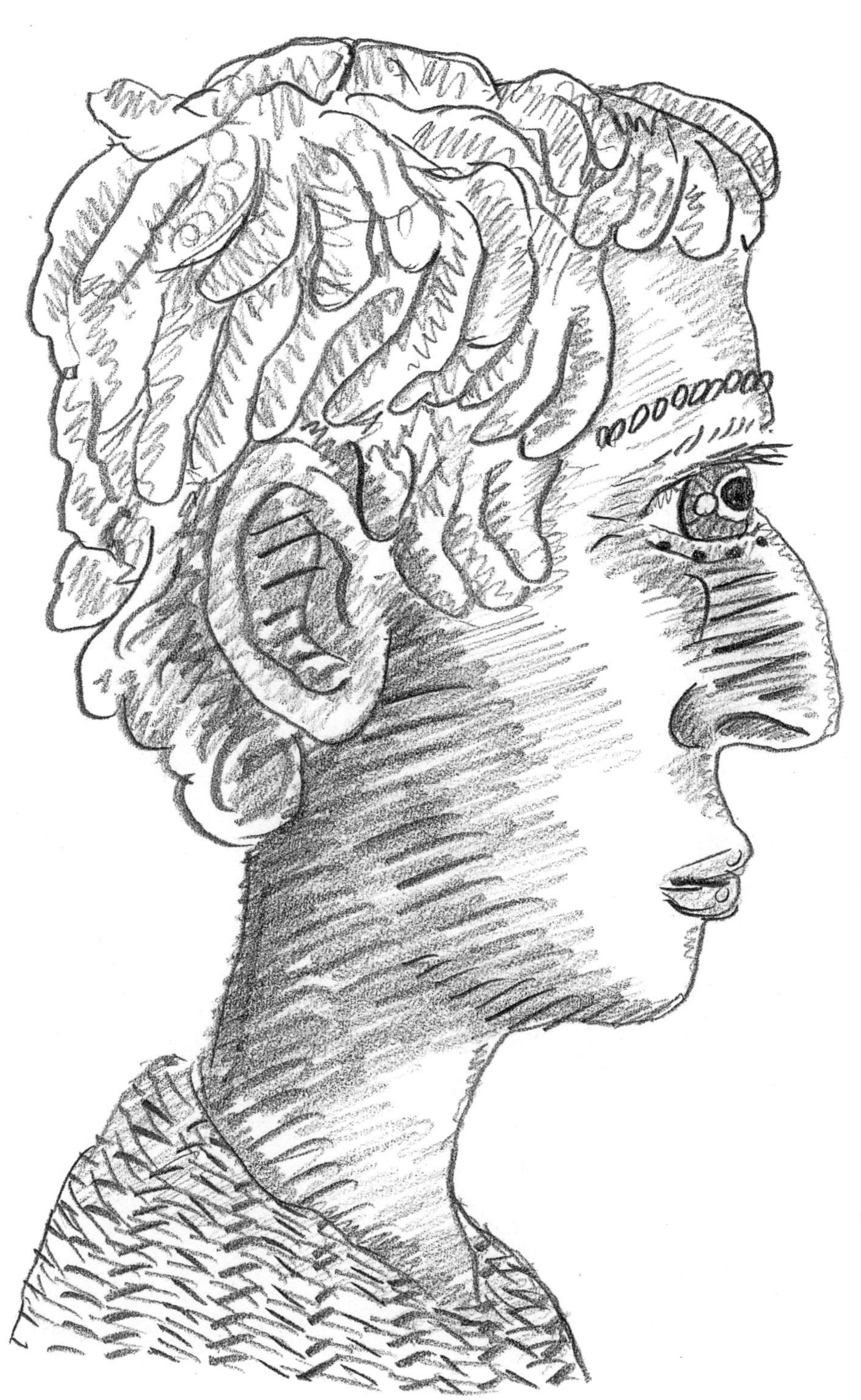

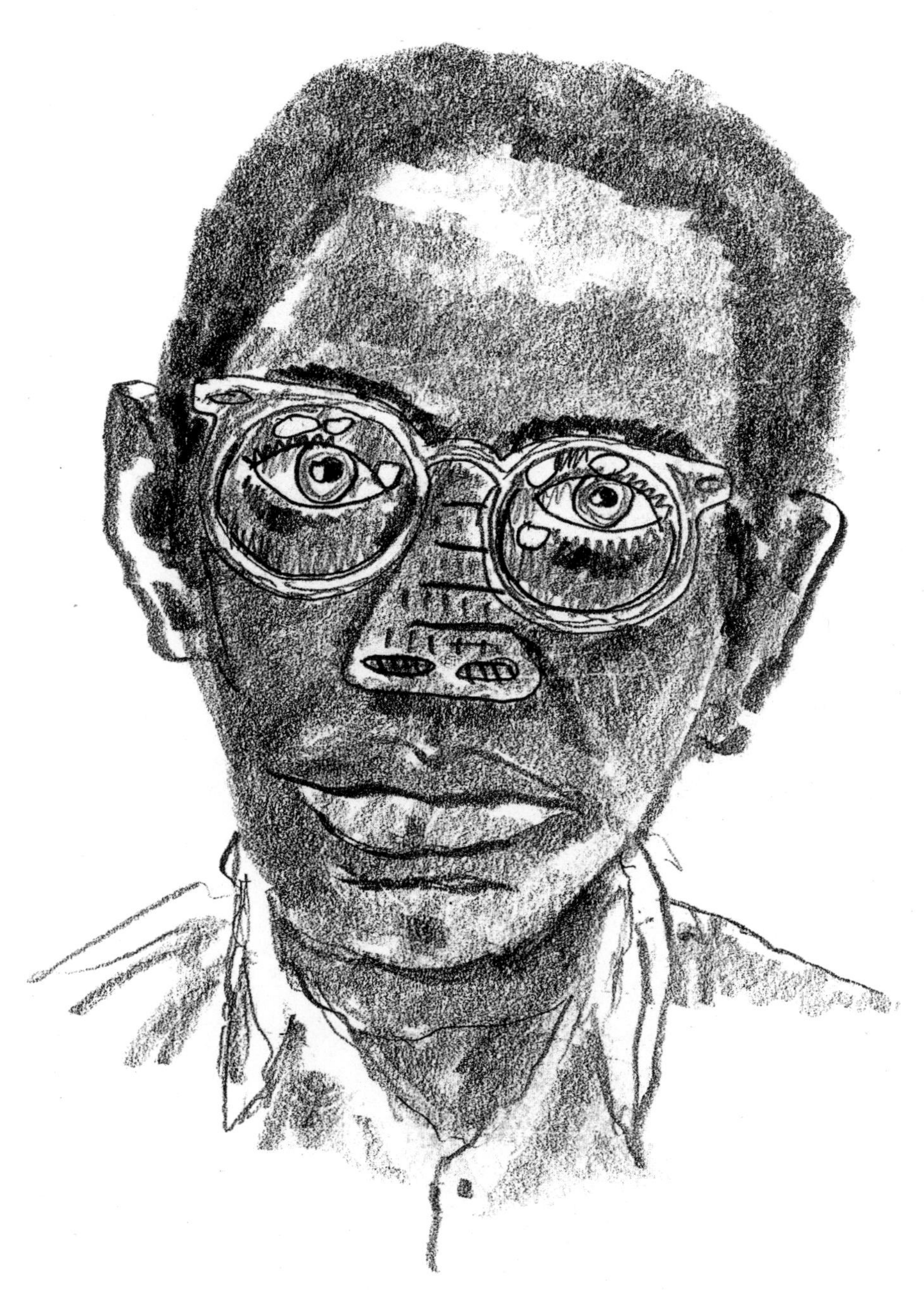

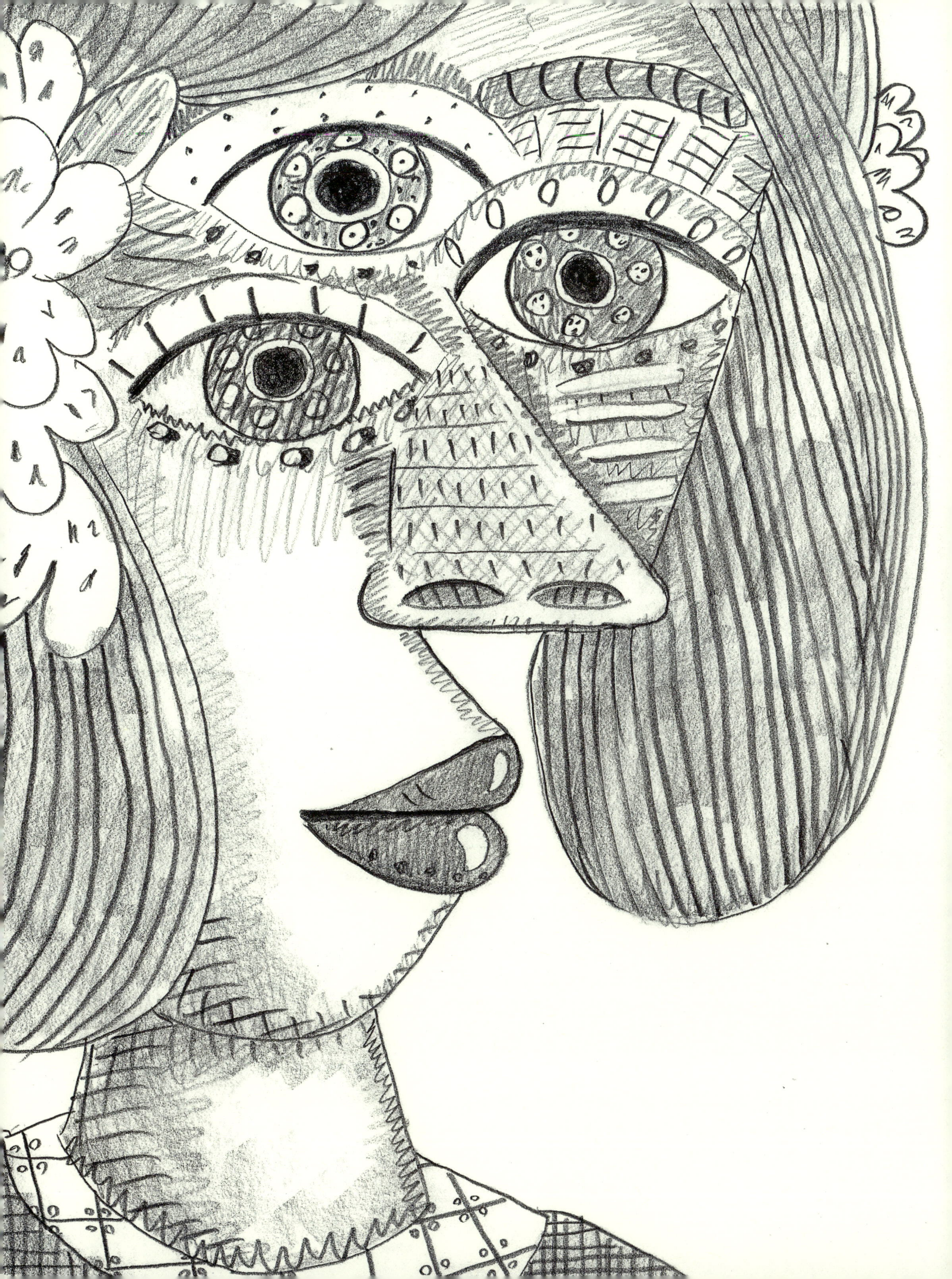

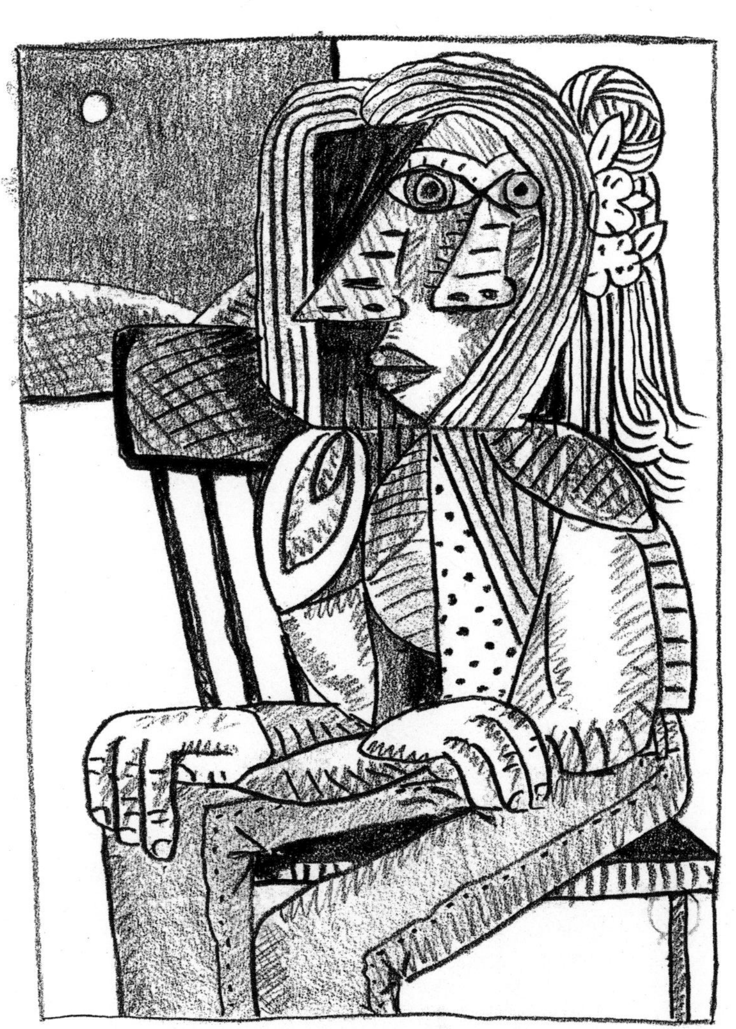

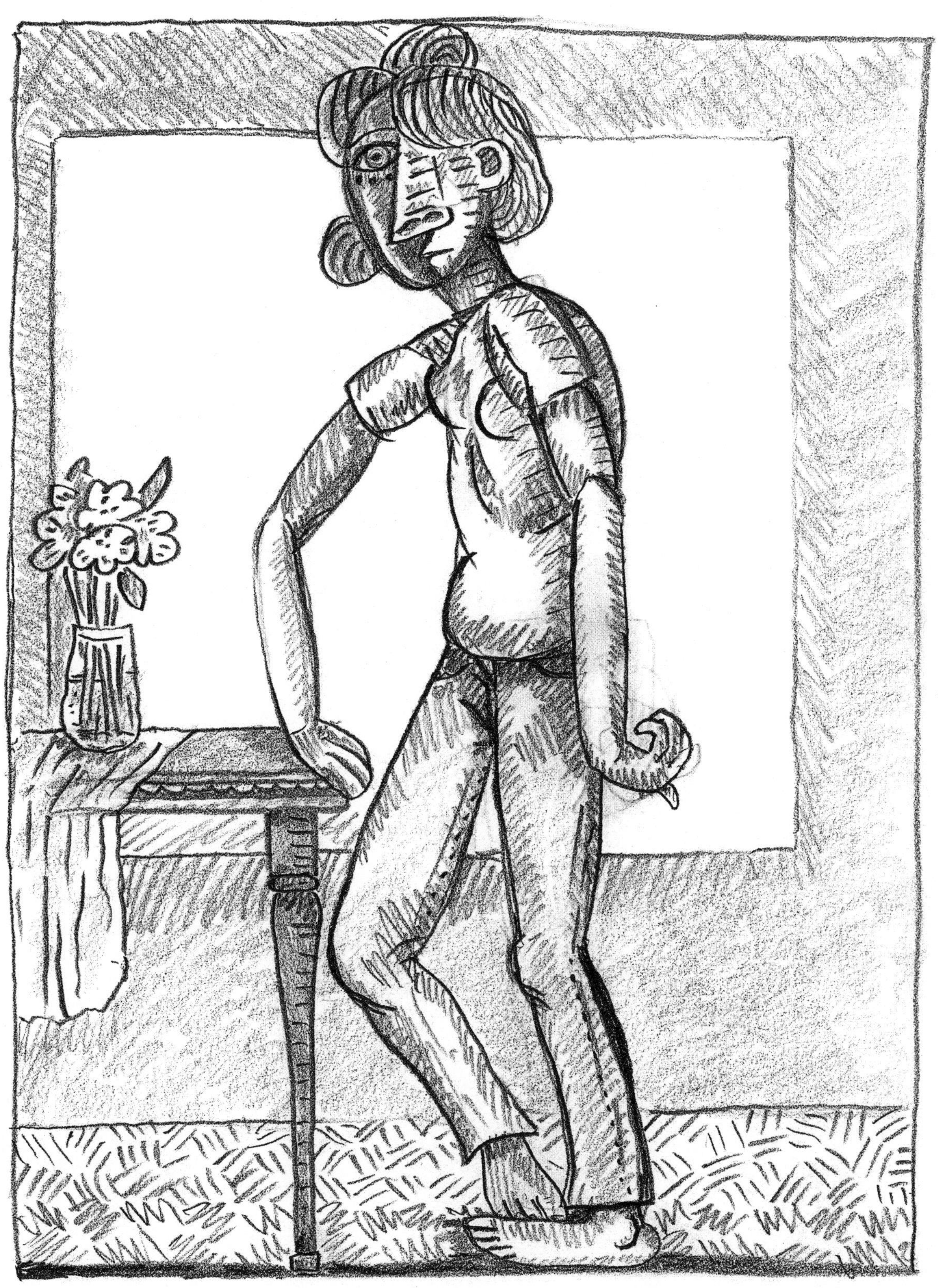

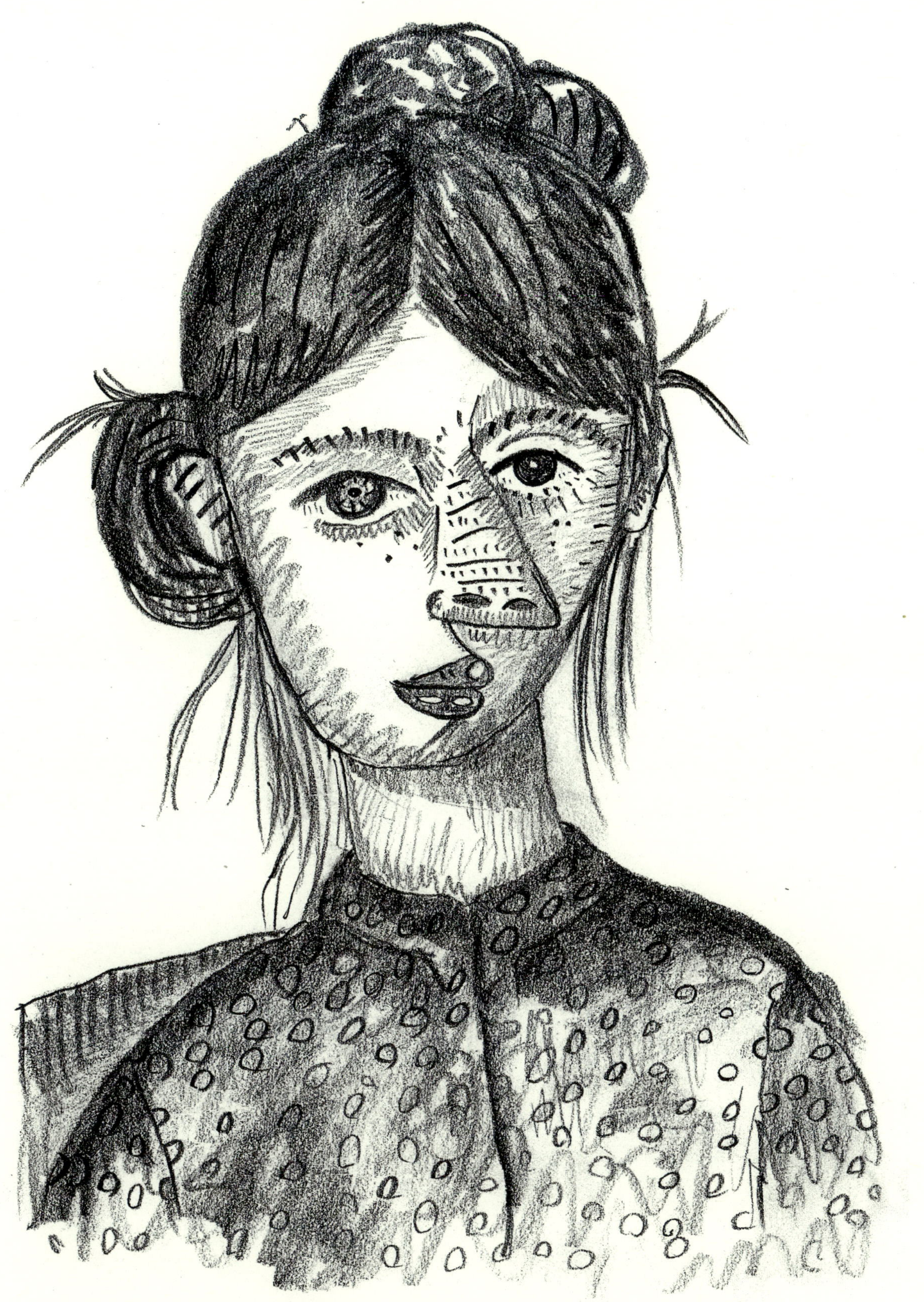

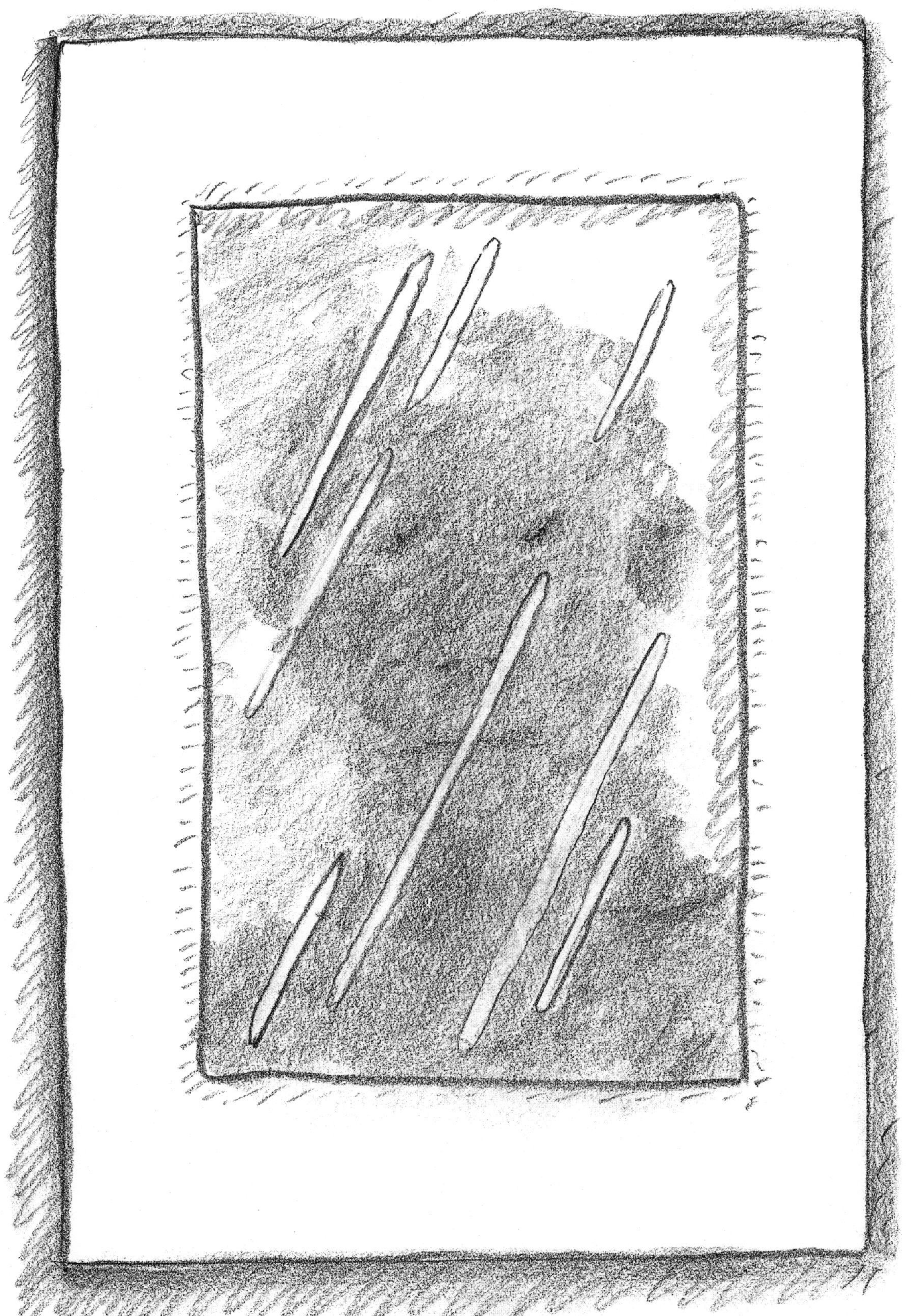

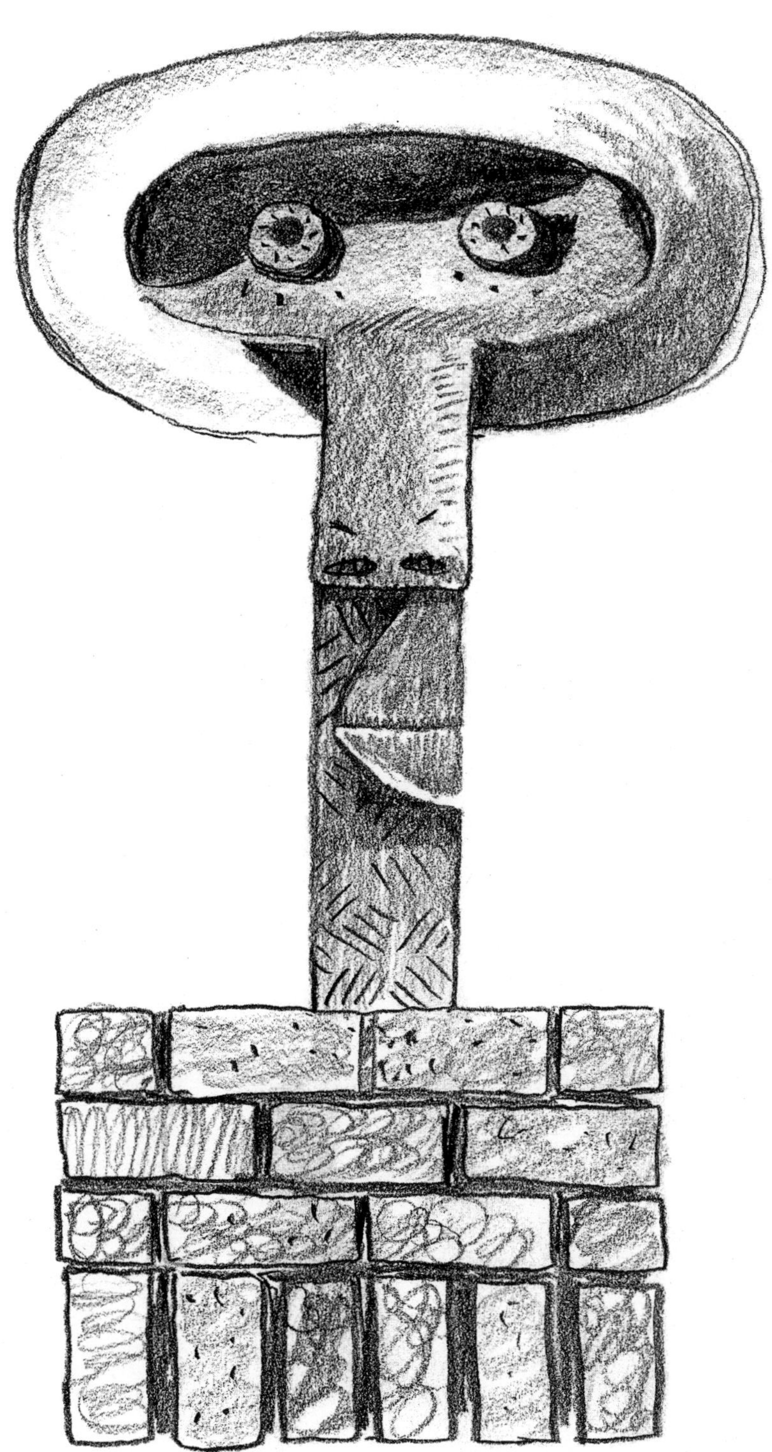

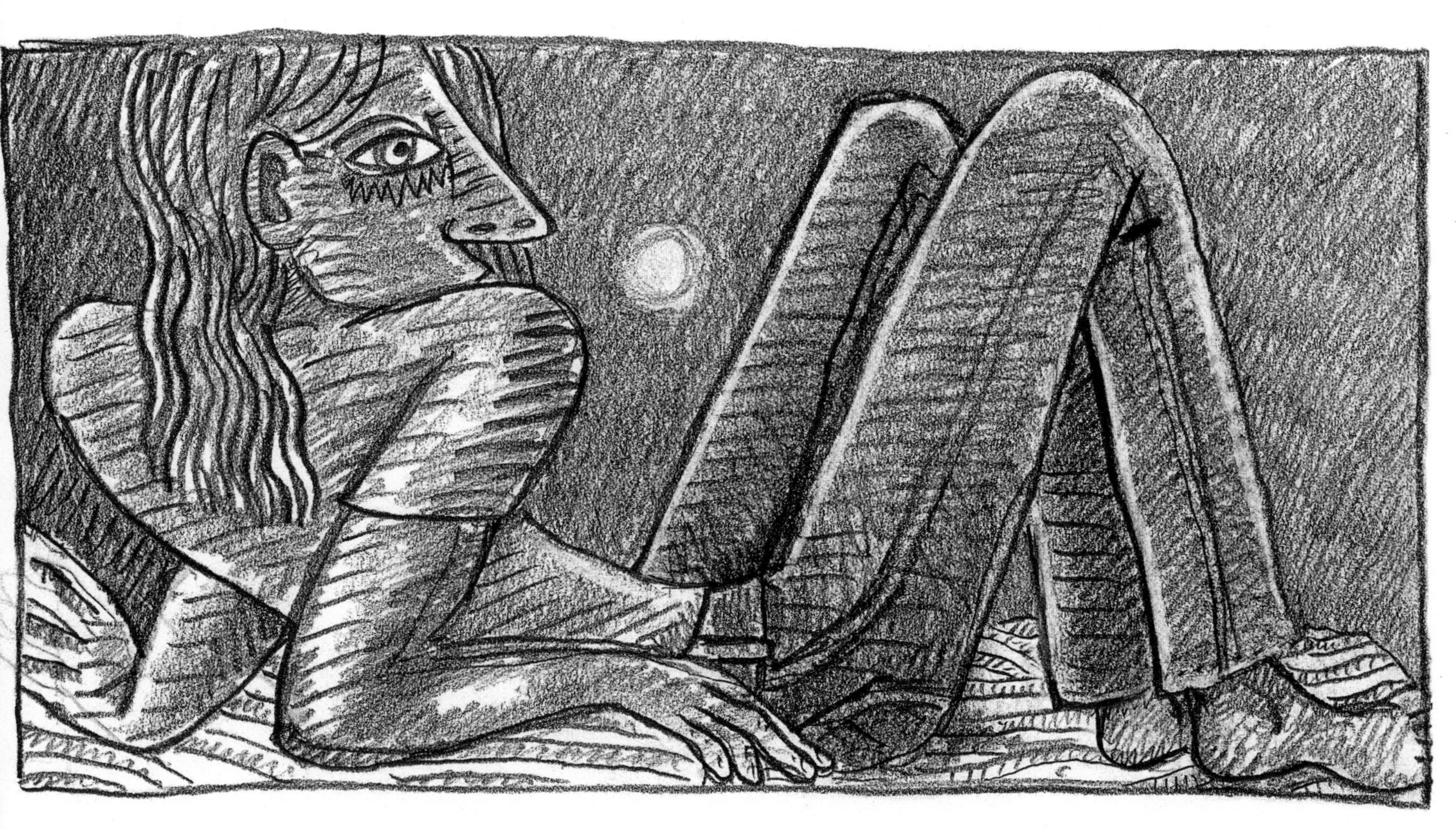

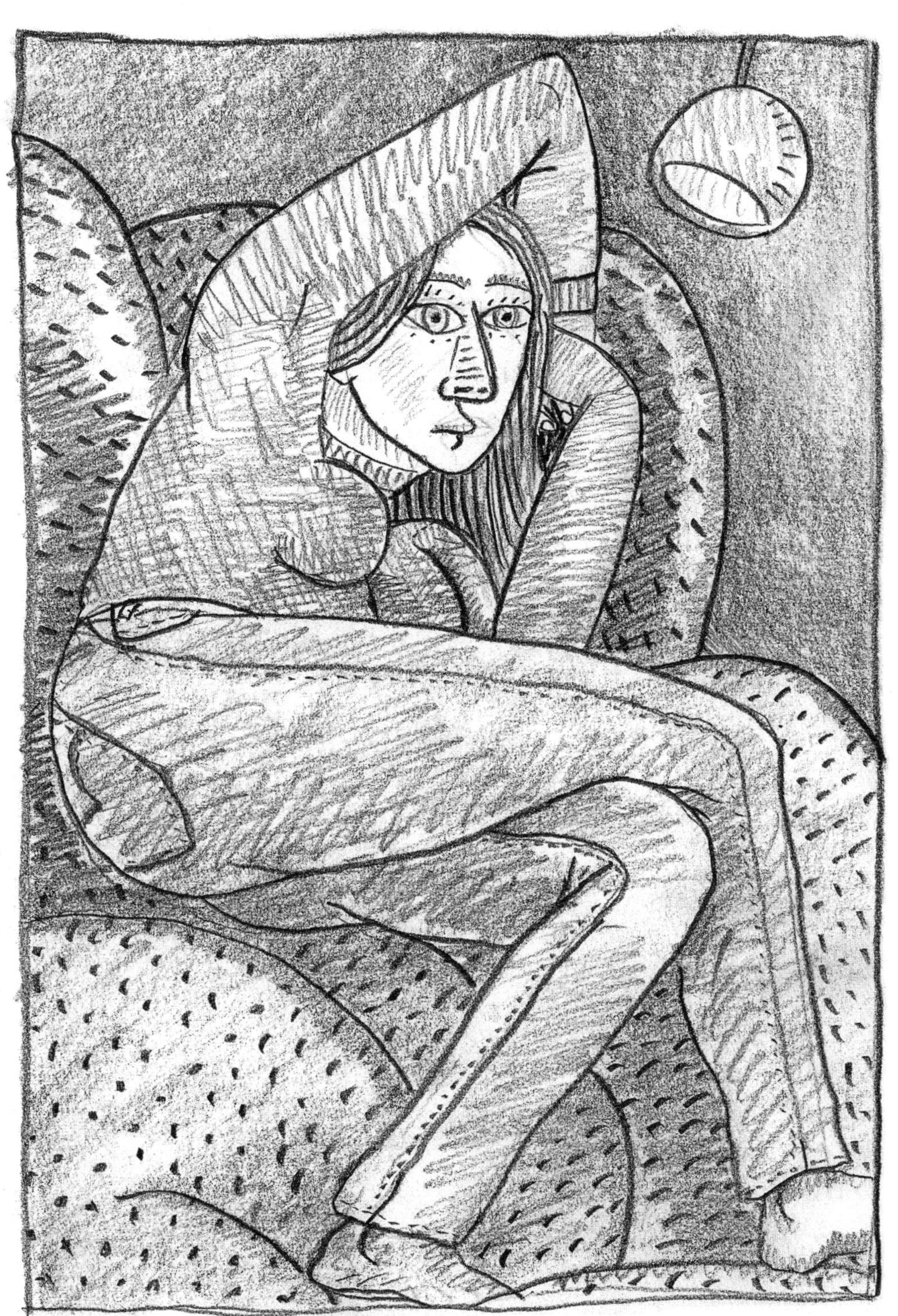

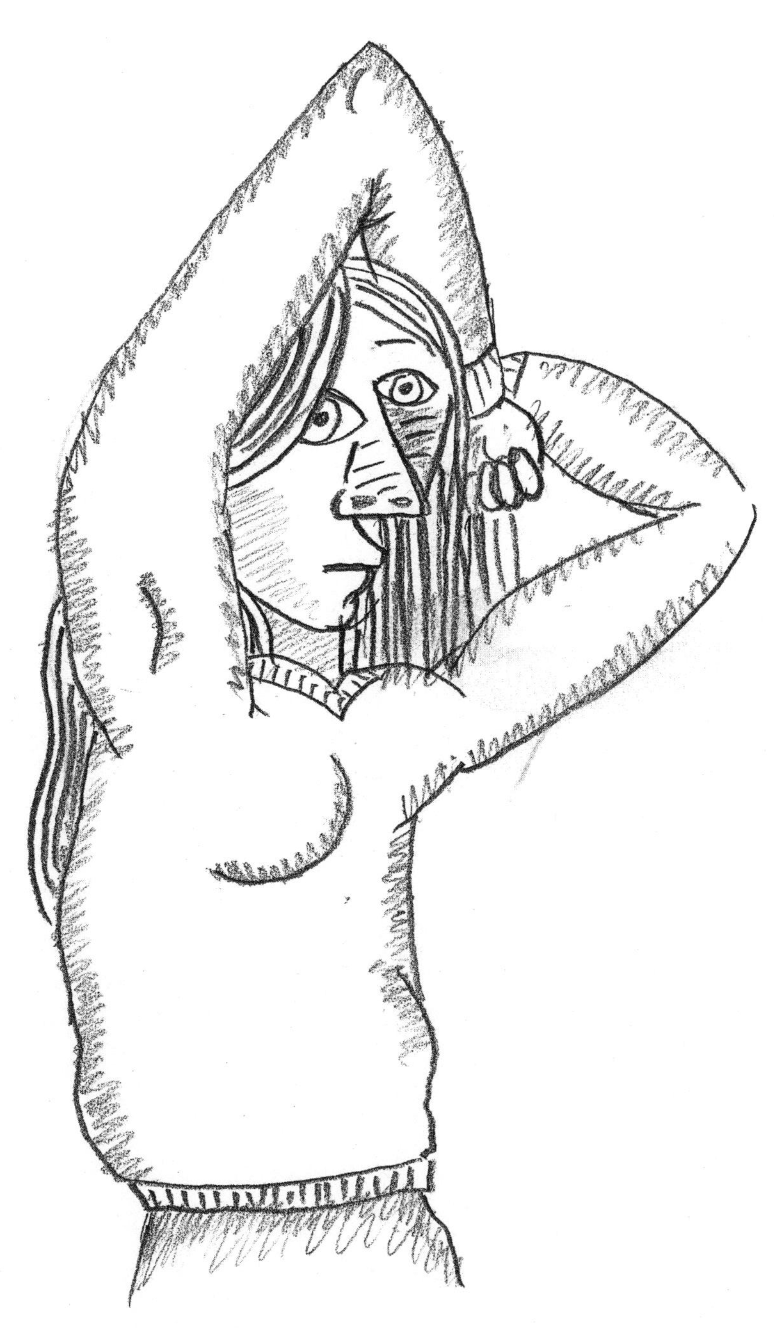

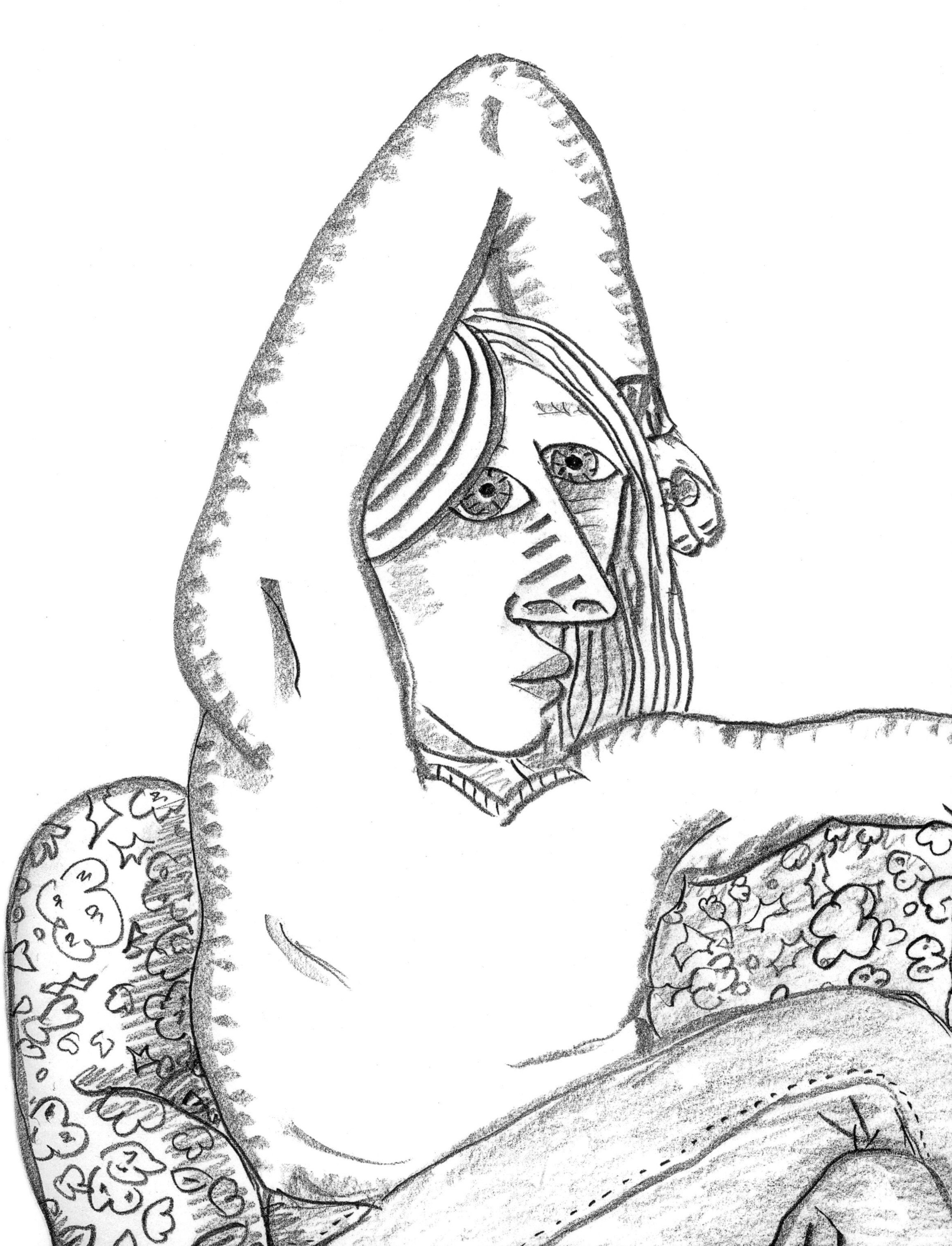

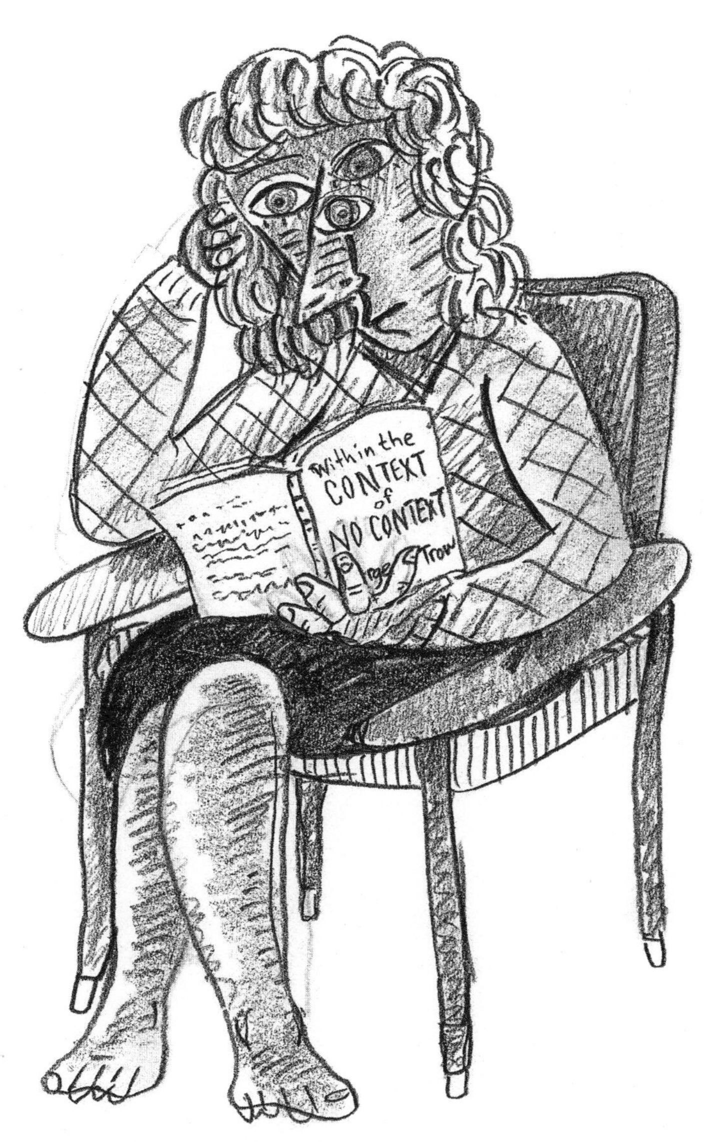

within the
CONTEXT
of
NO CONTEXT
George Trow

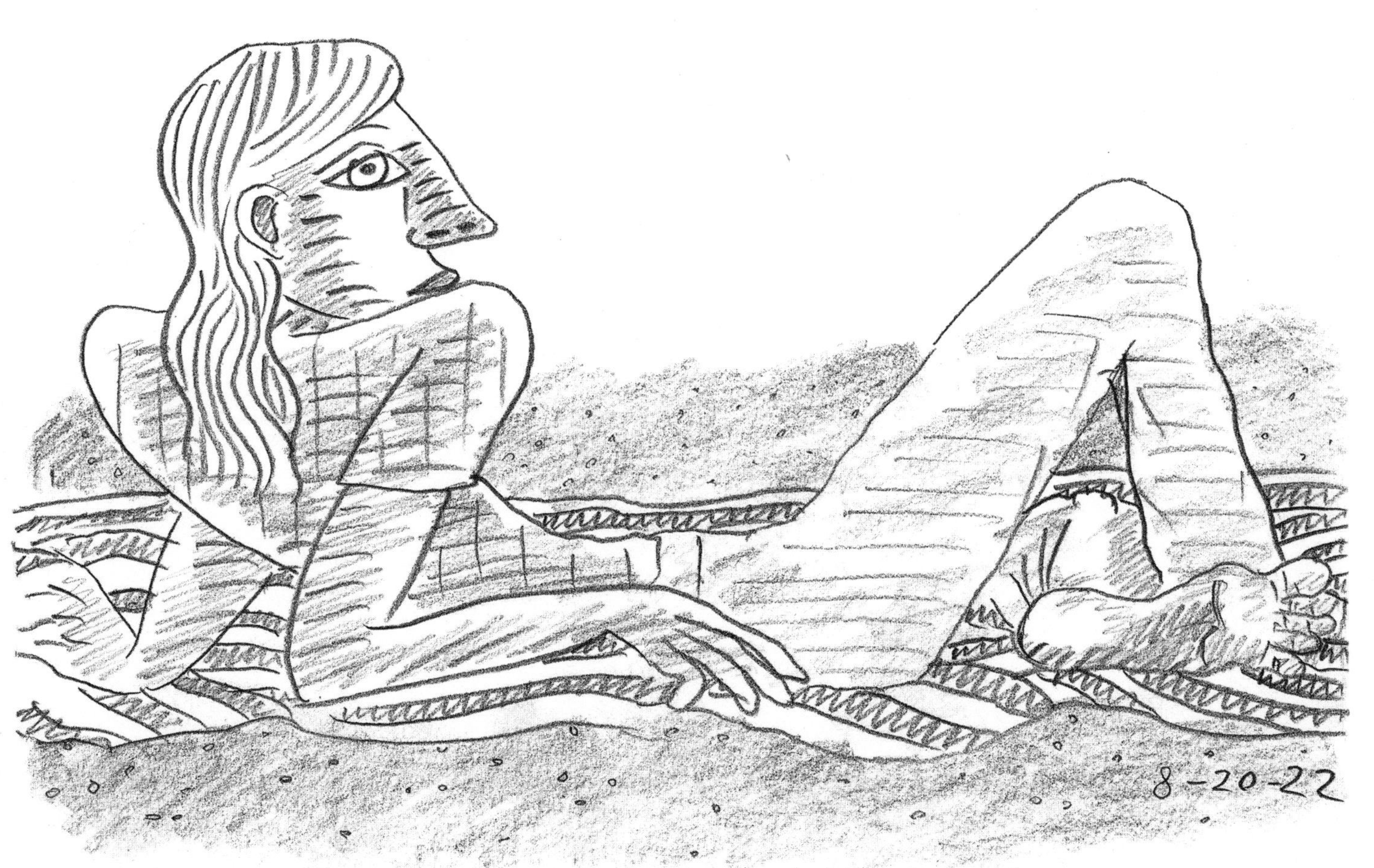
8-20-22

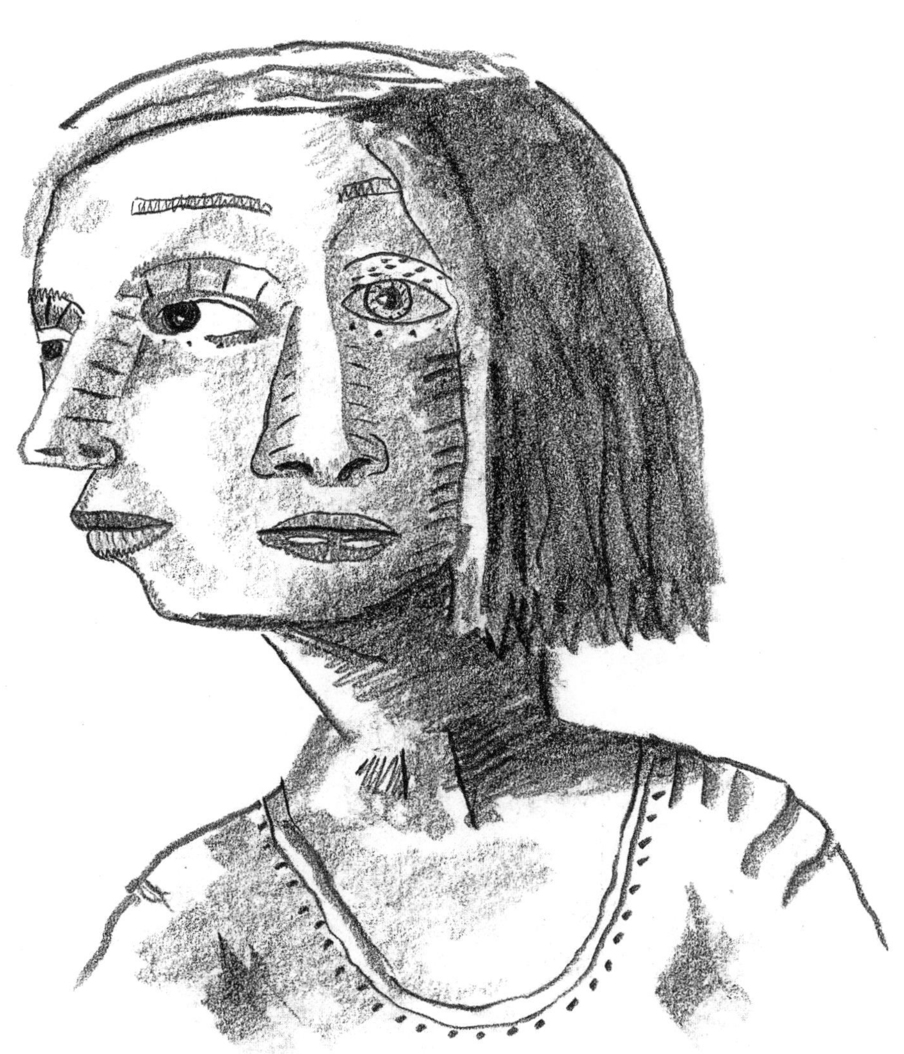

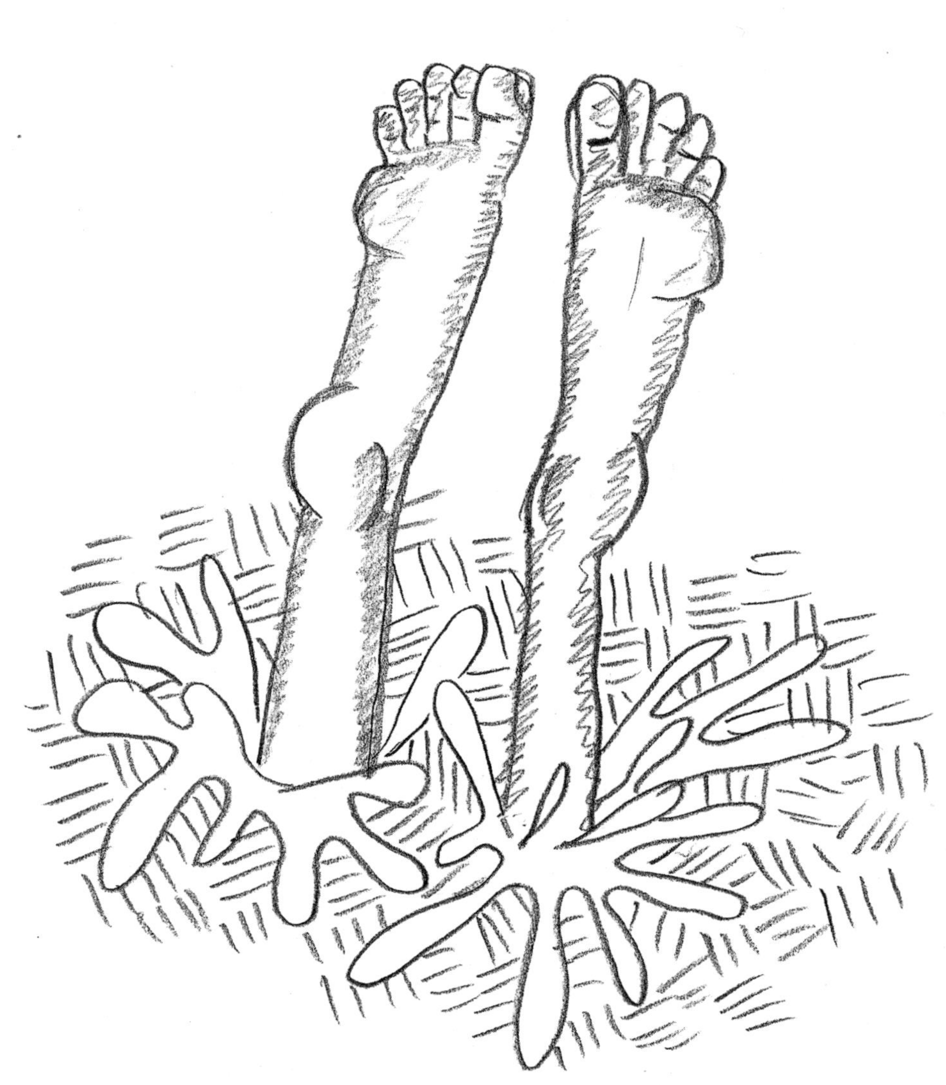

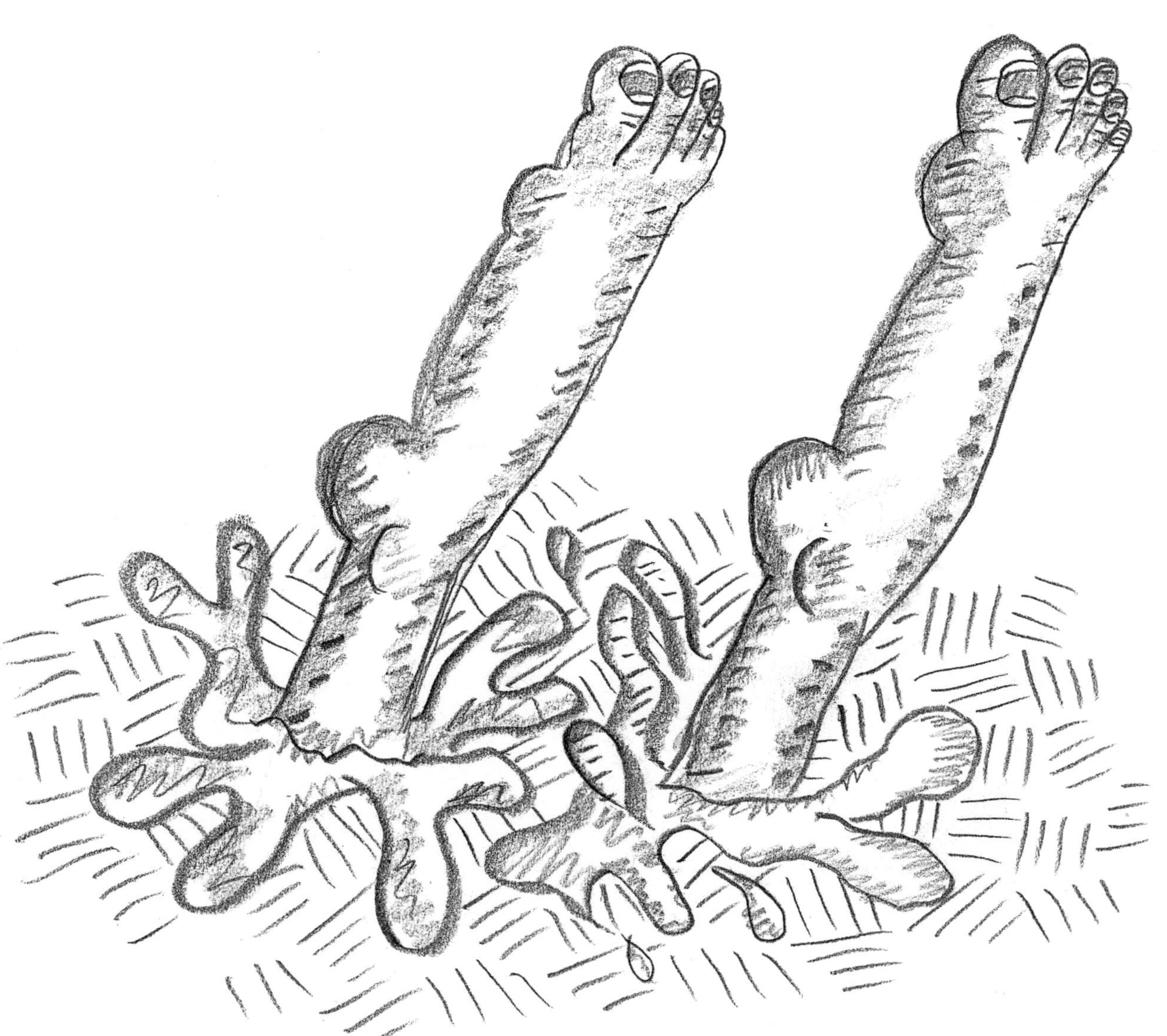

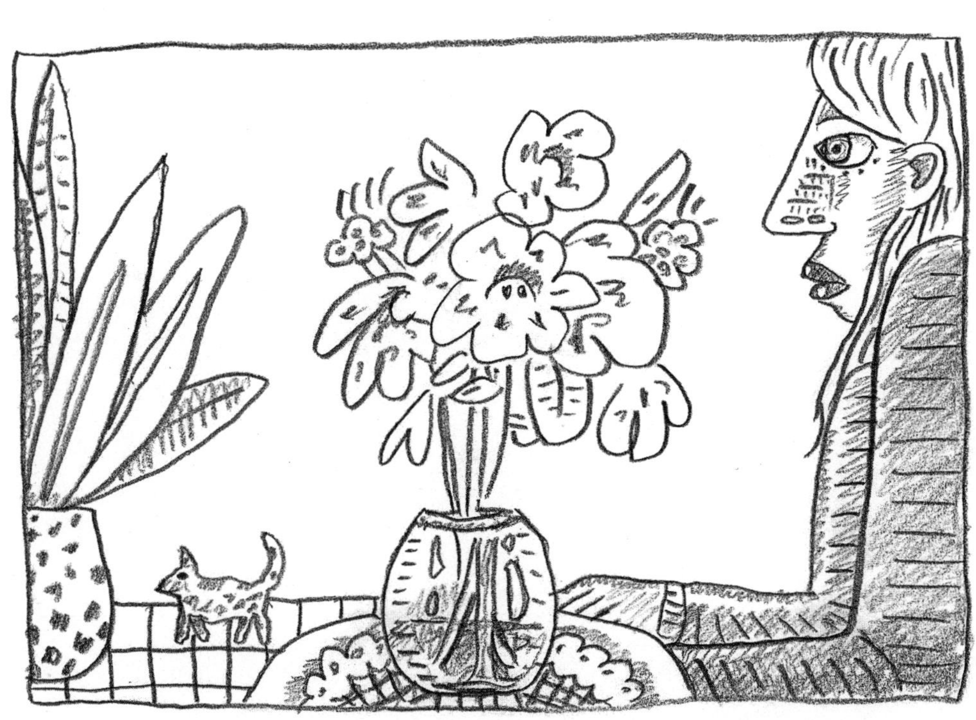

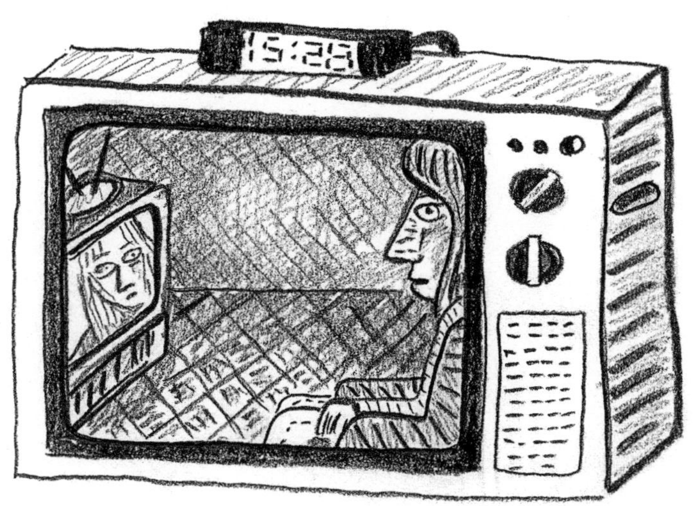

15:28

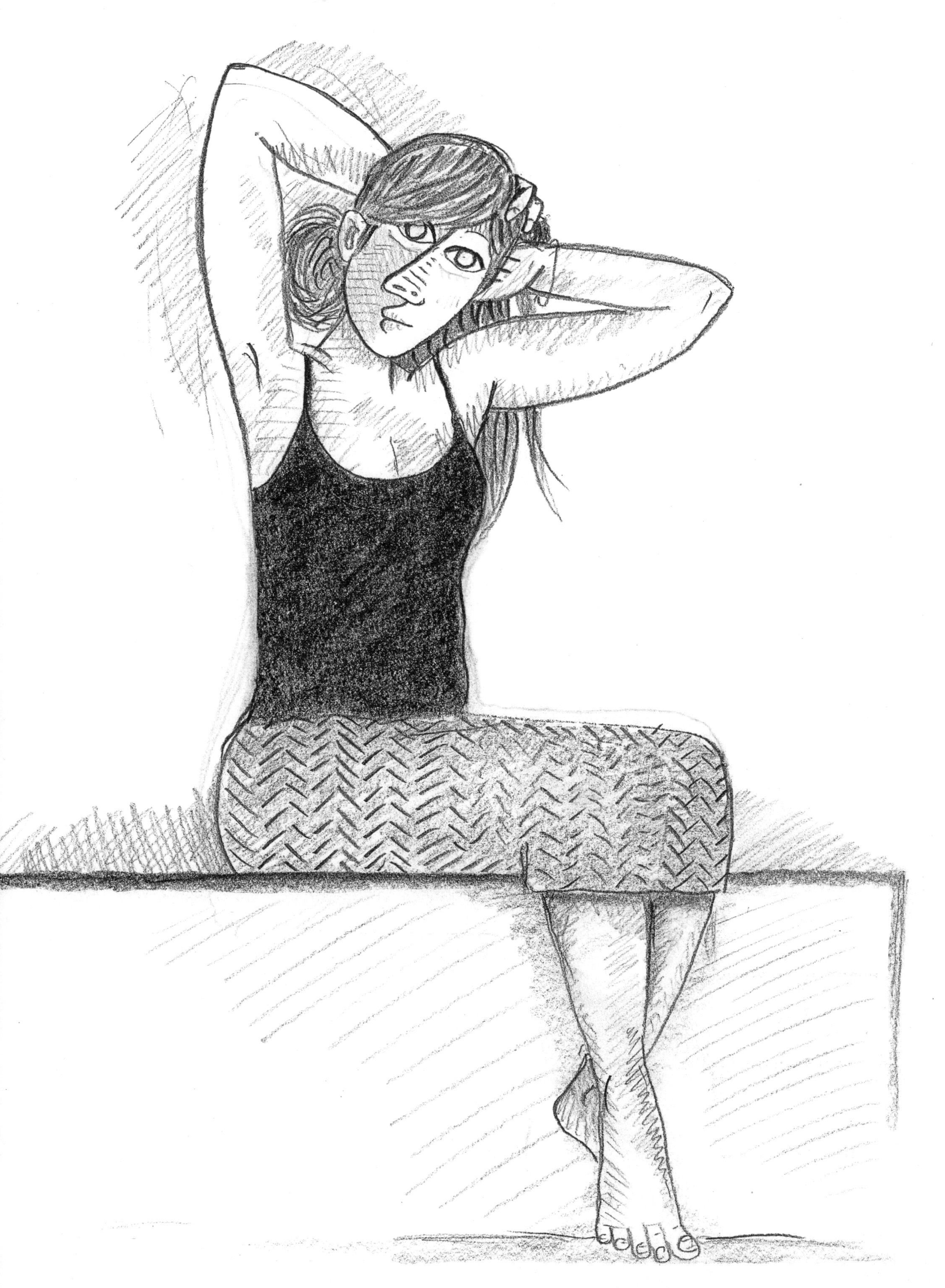

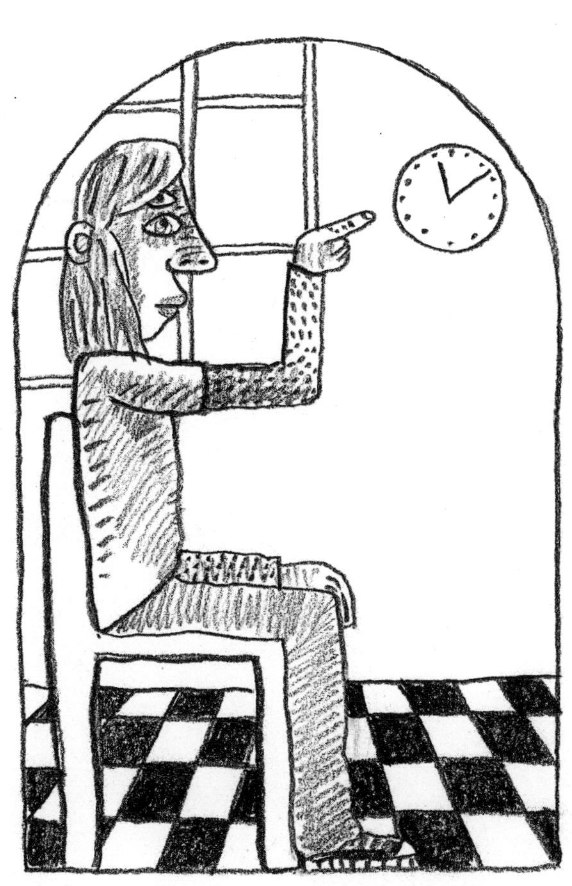

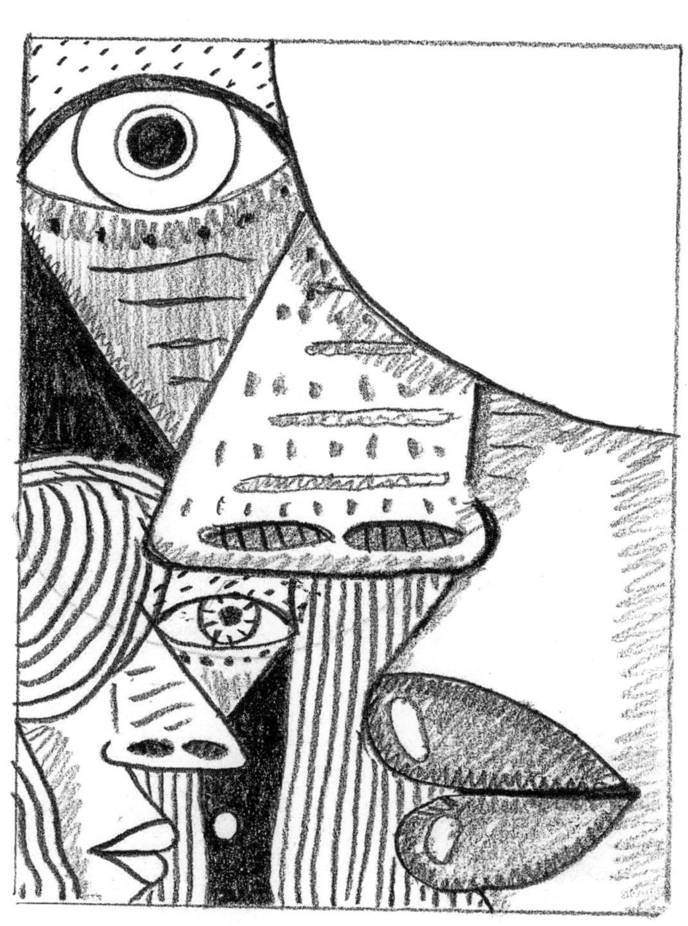

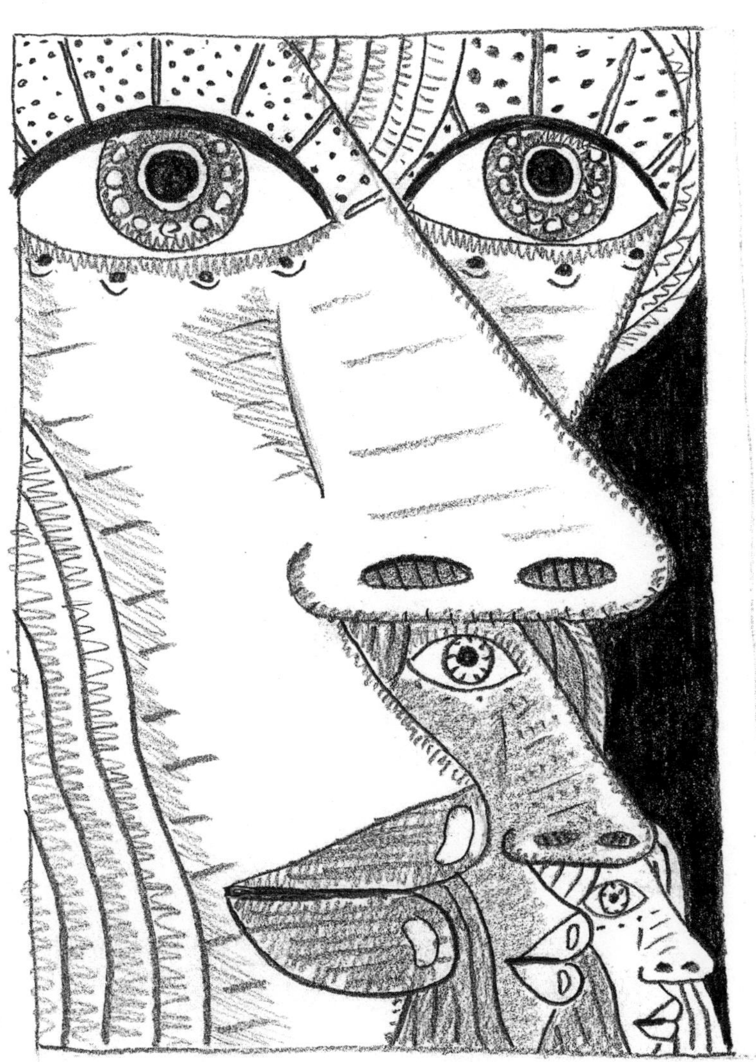

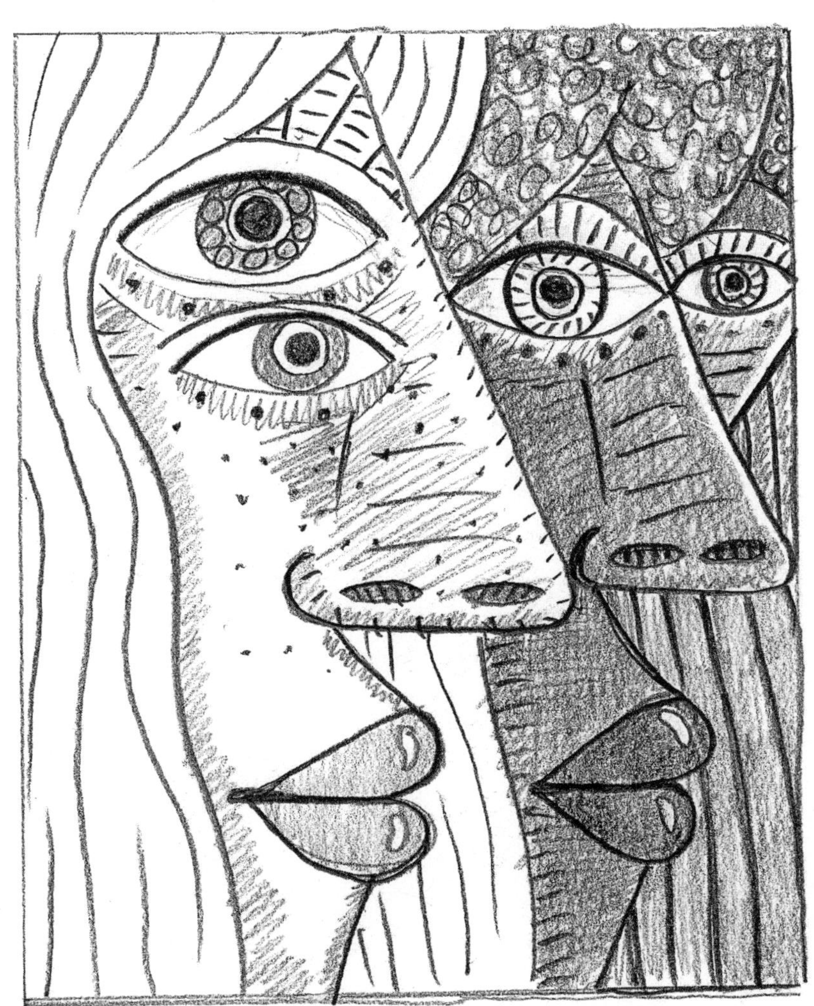

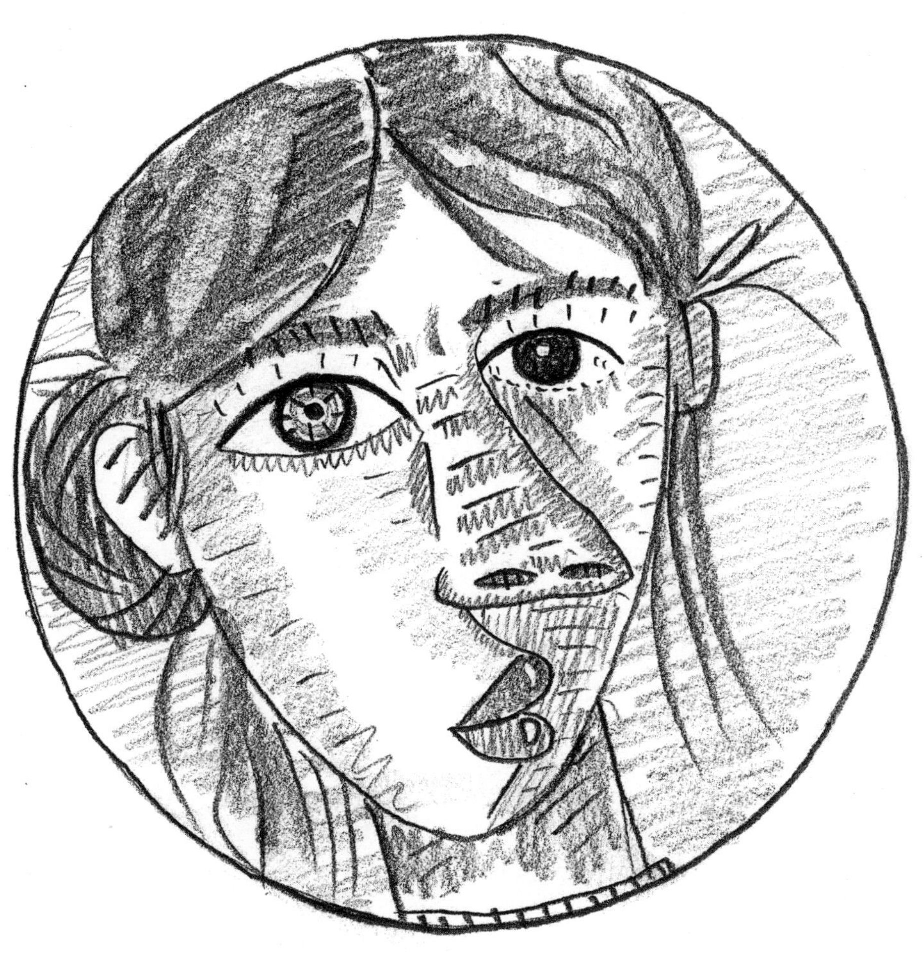

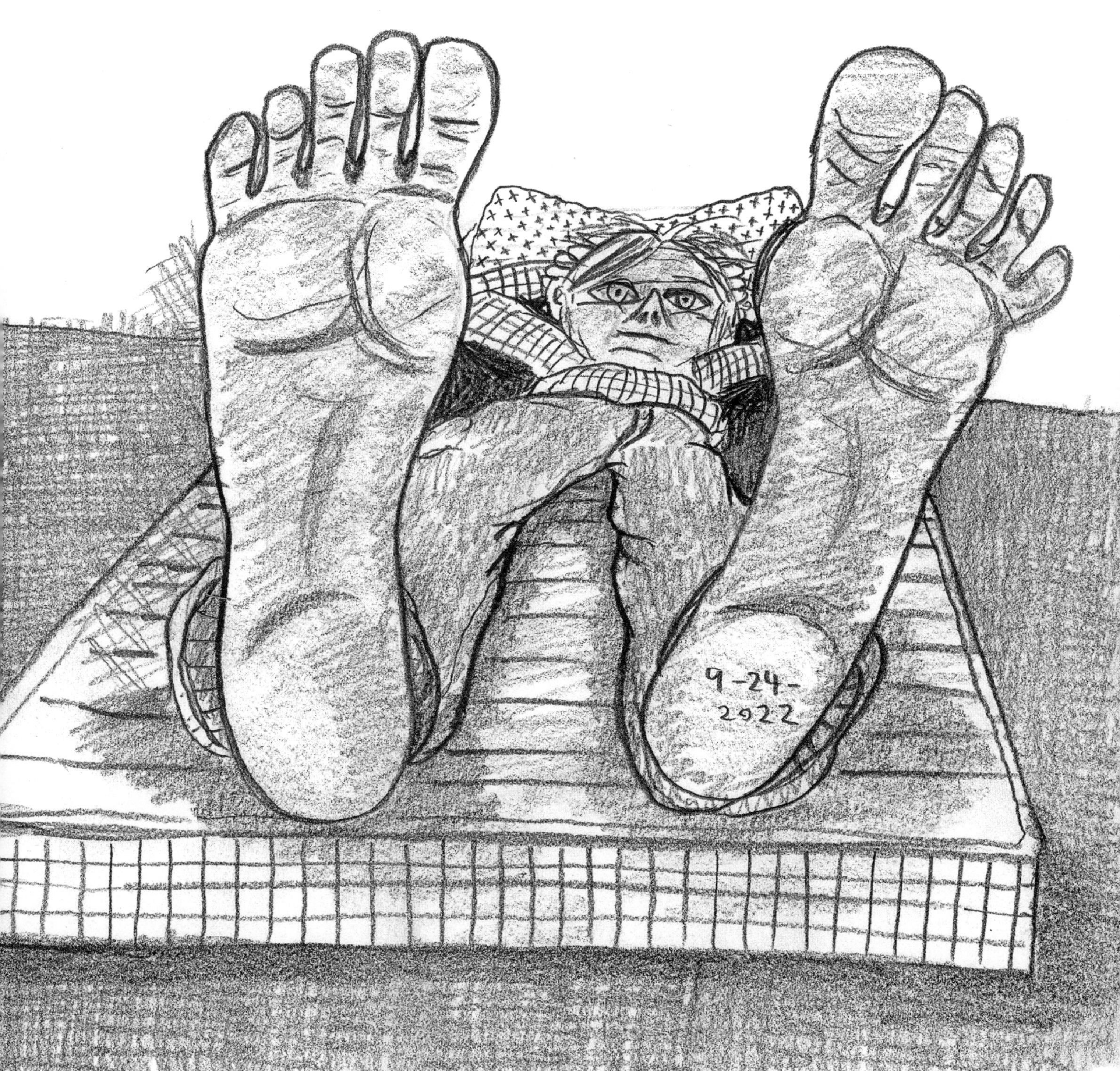
9-24-
2022

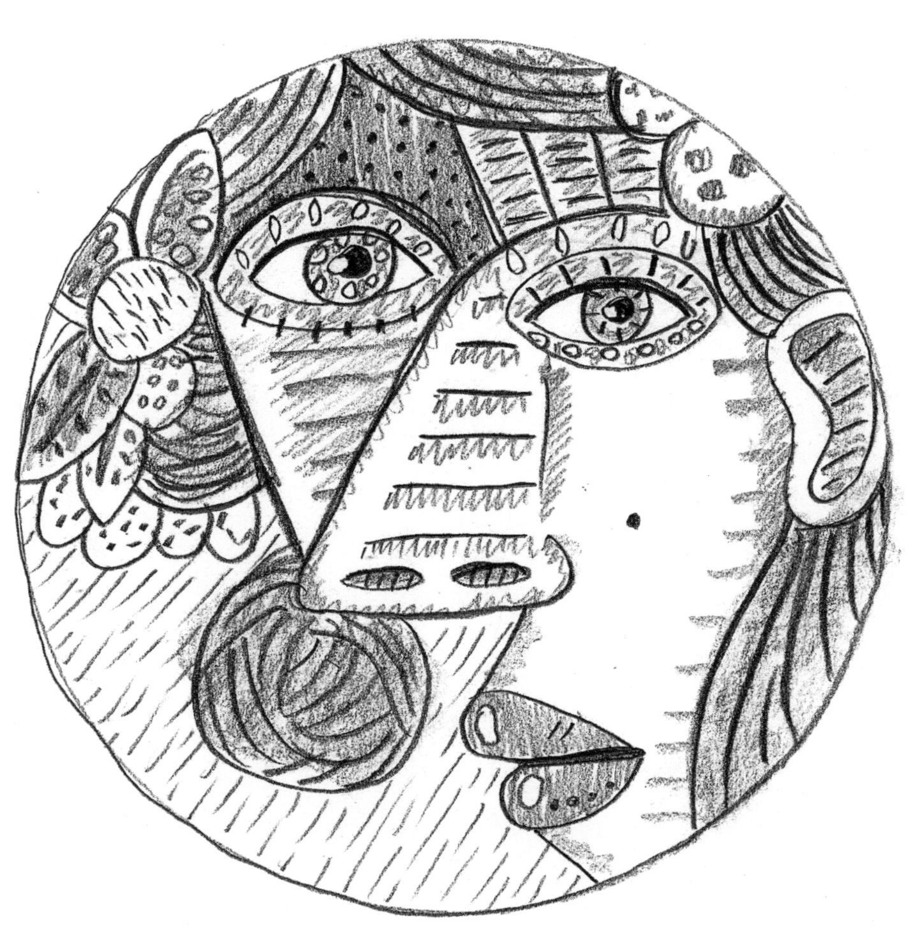

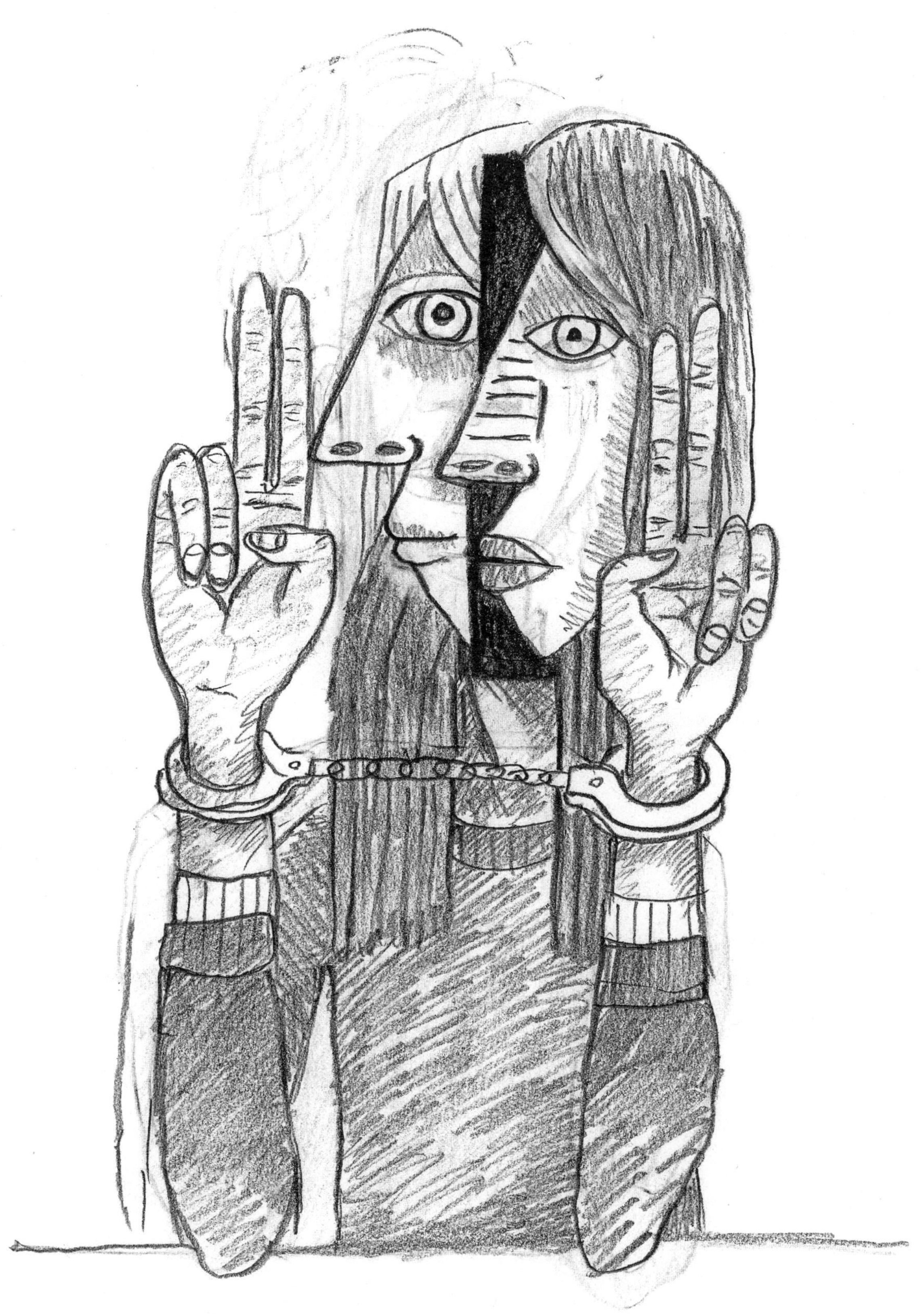

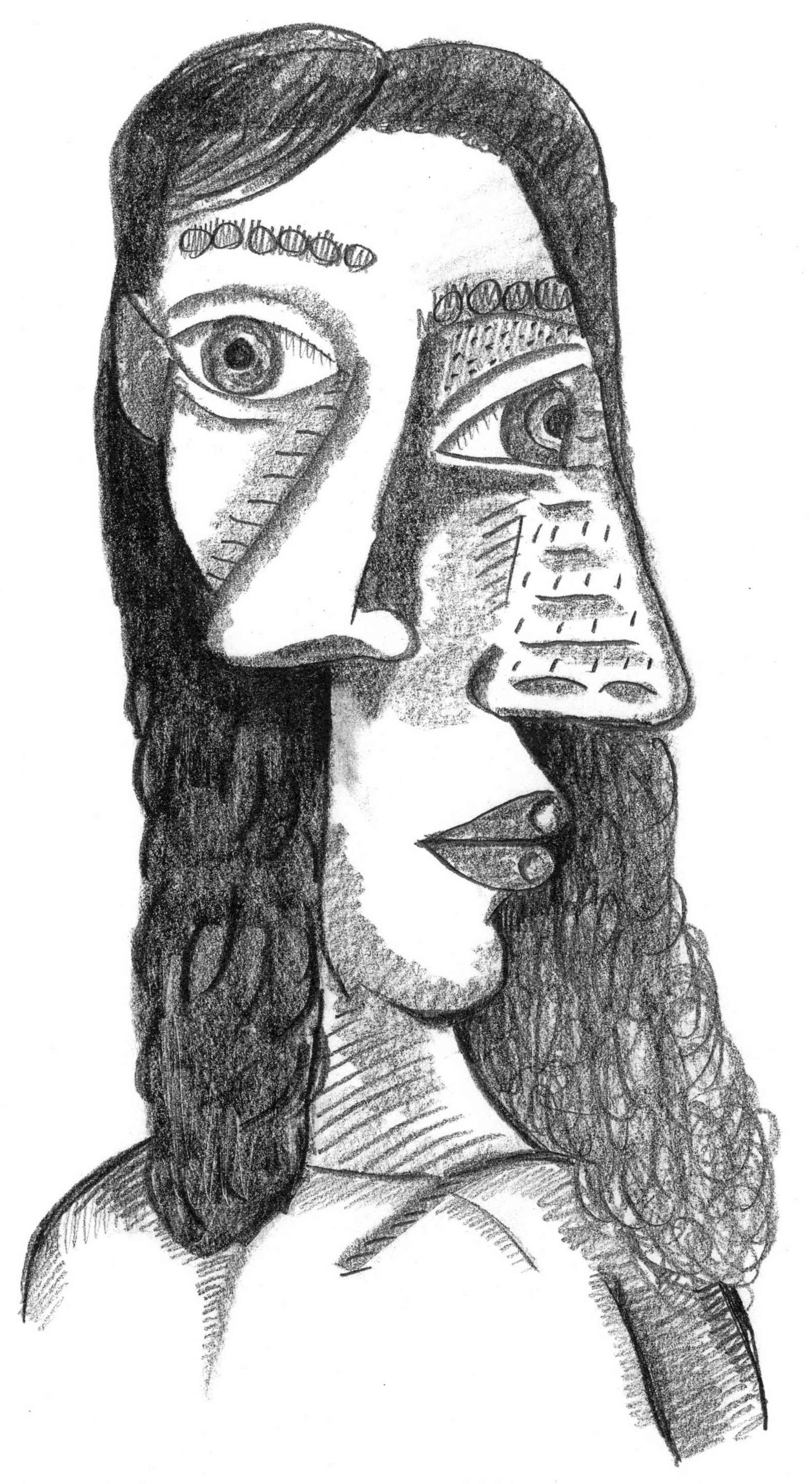

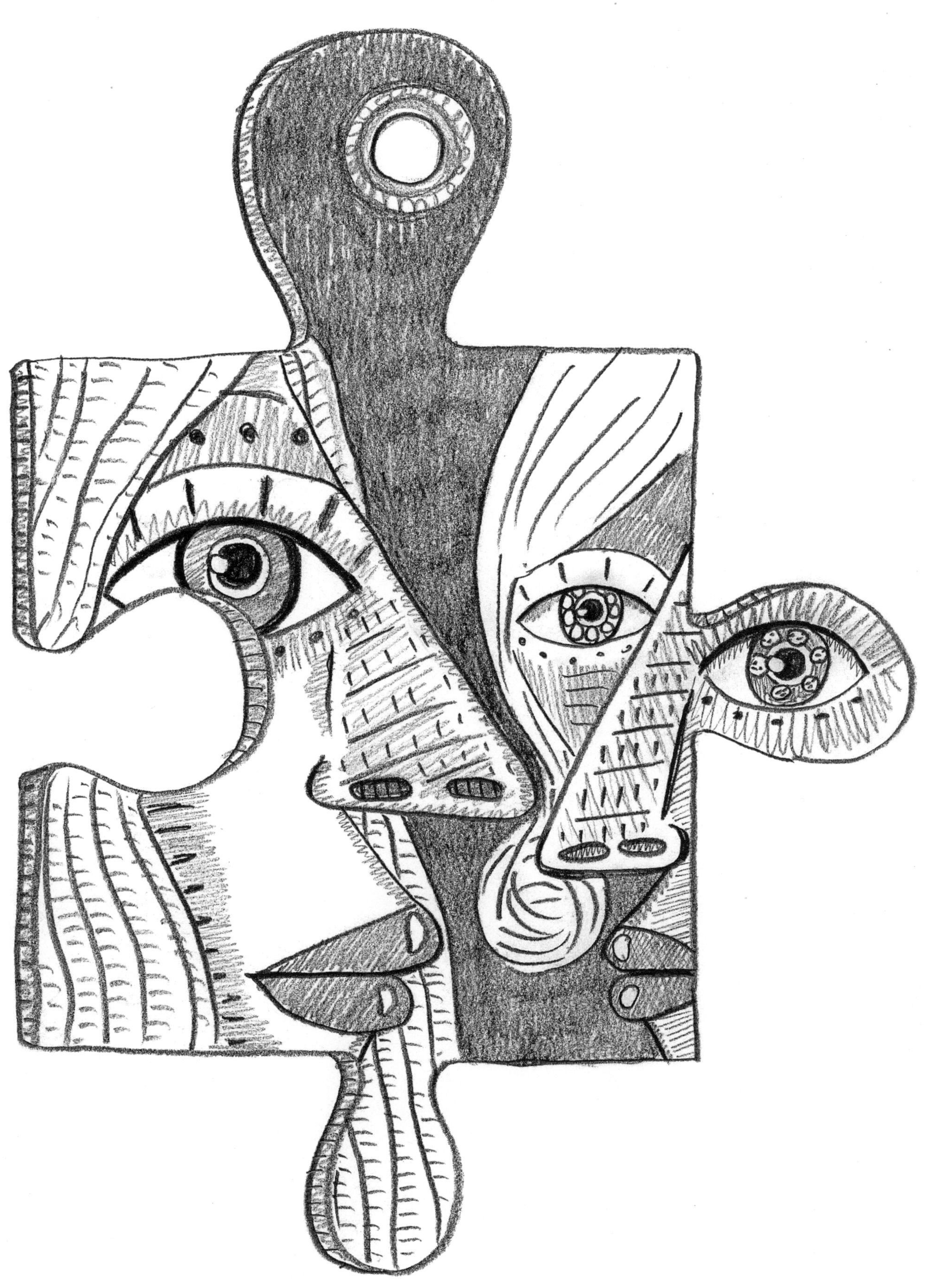

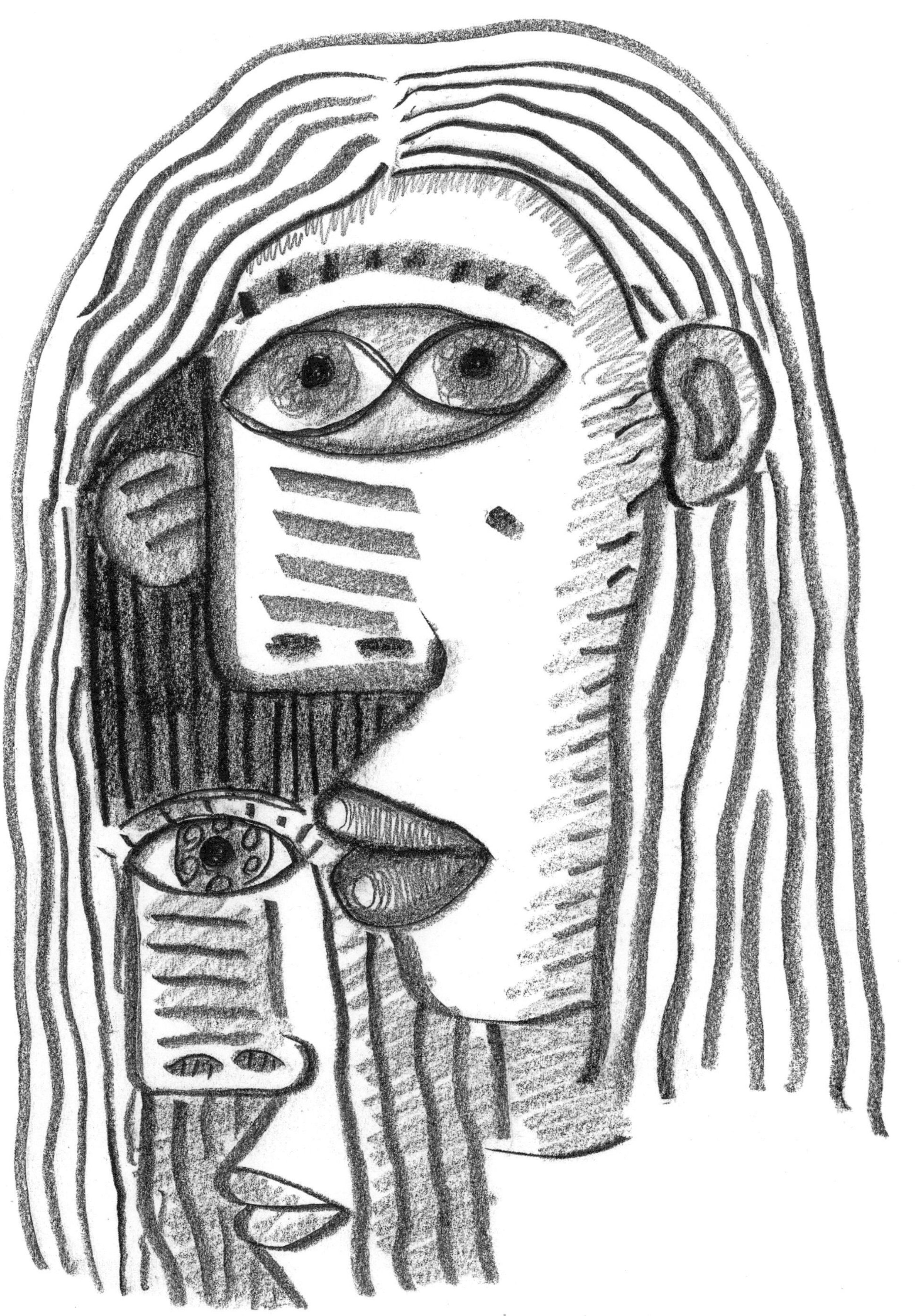

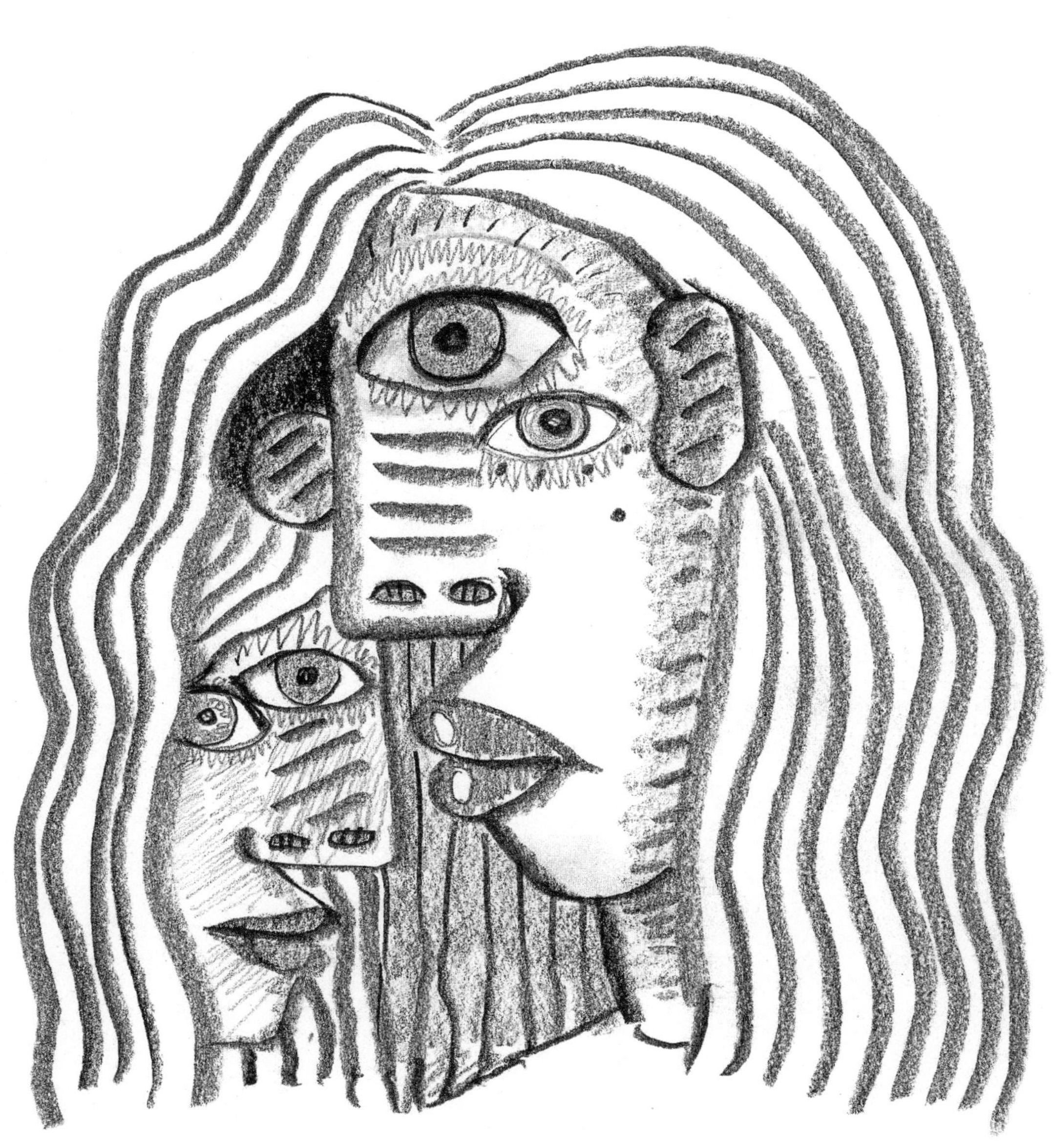

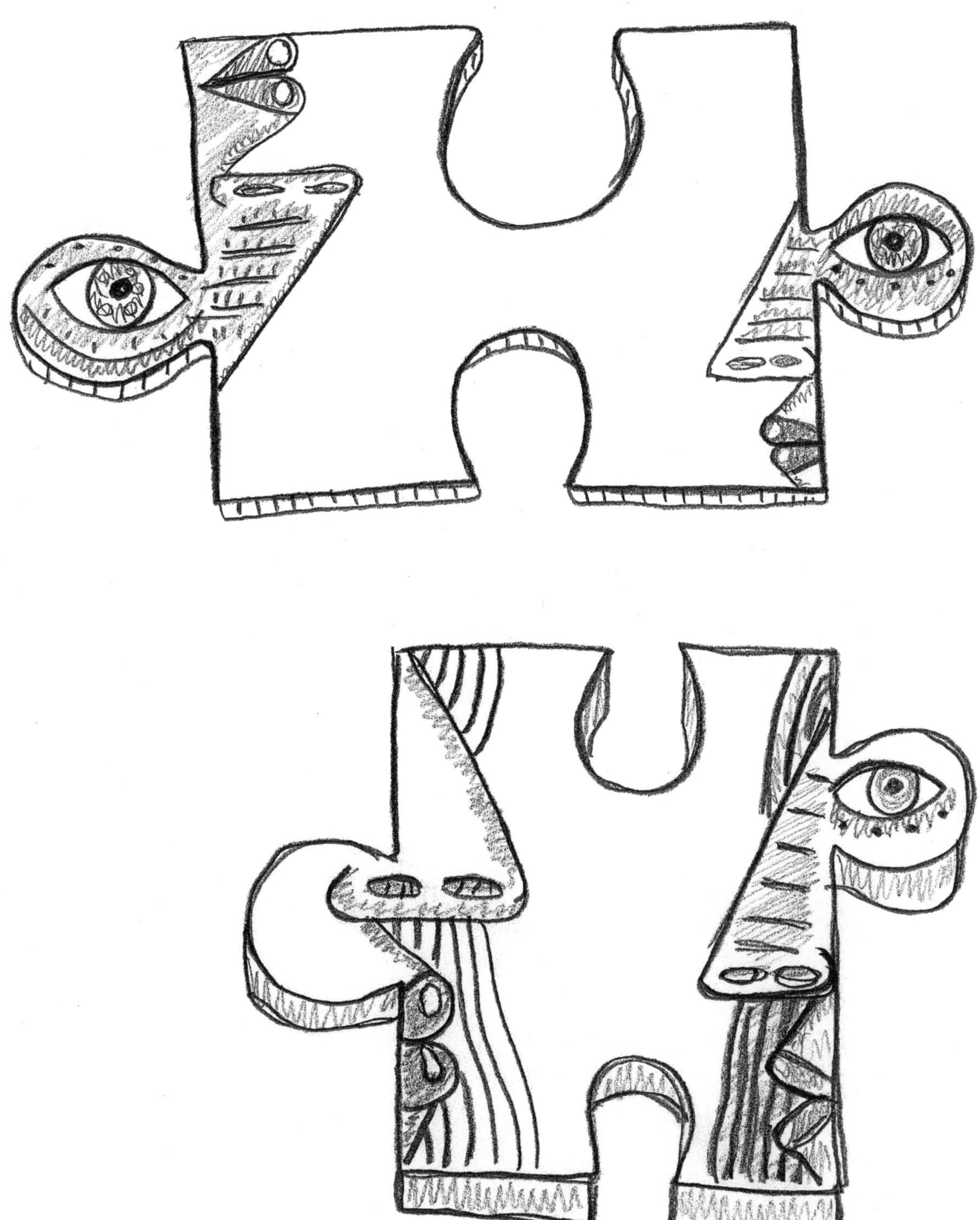

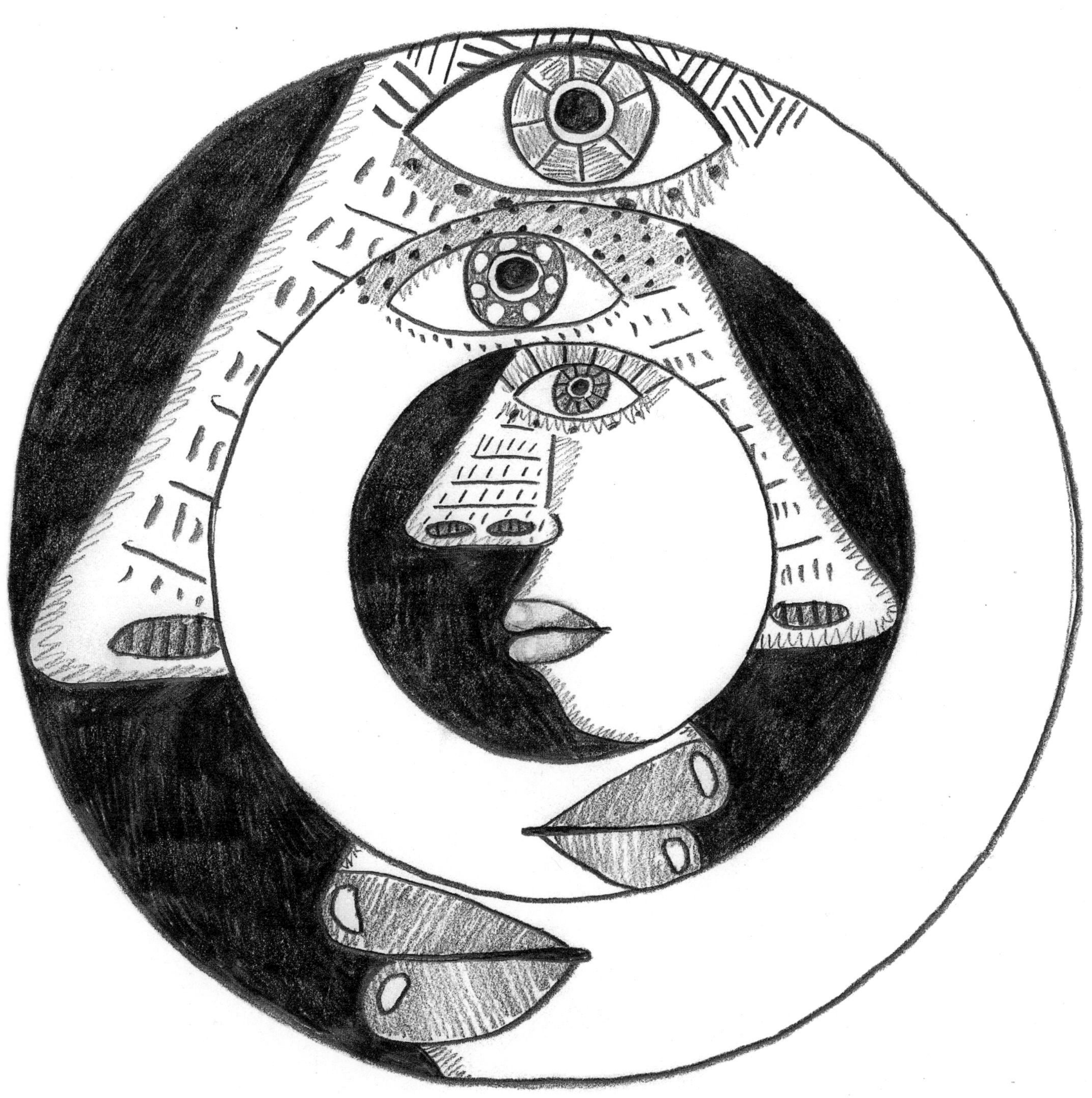

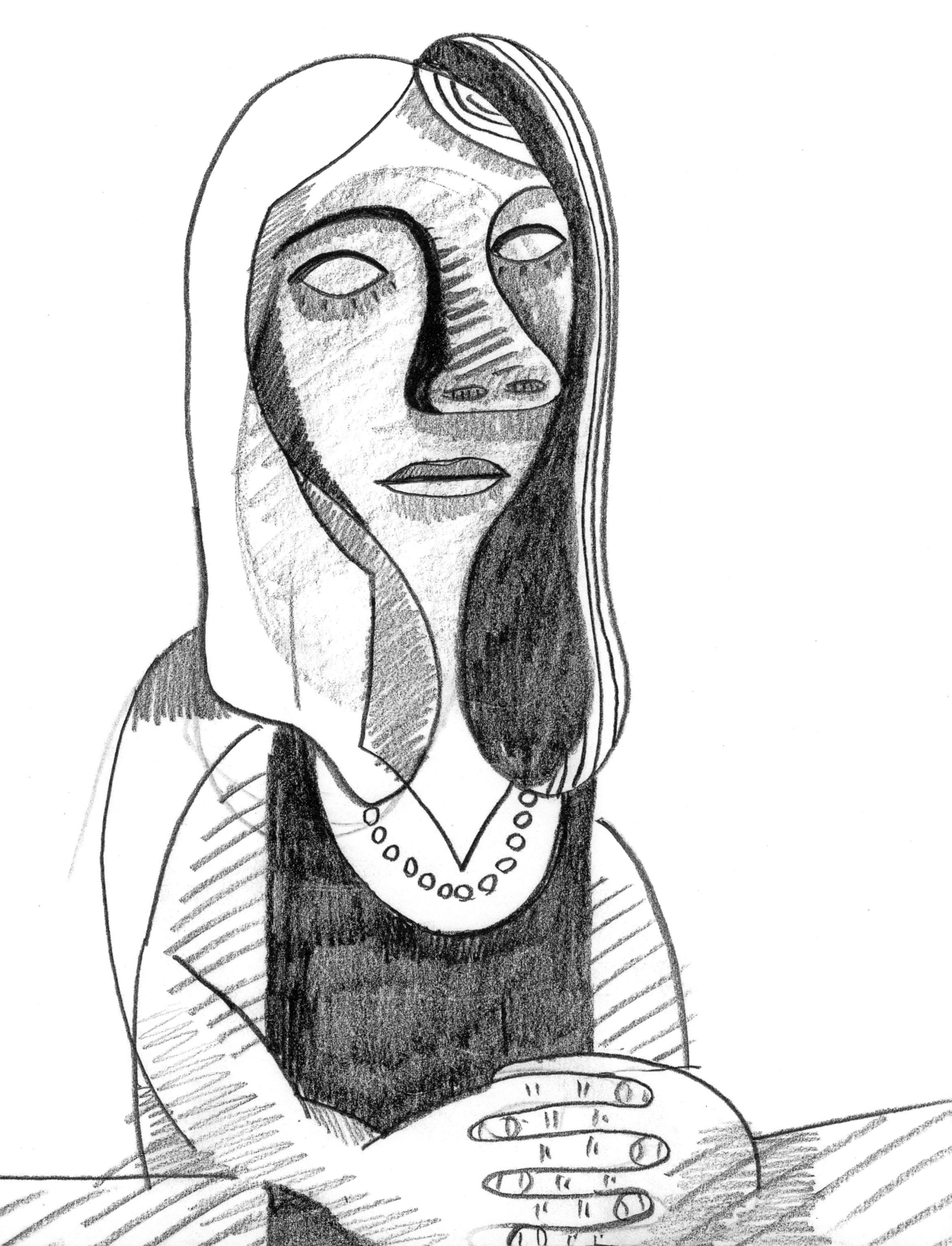

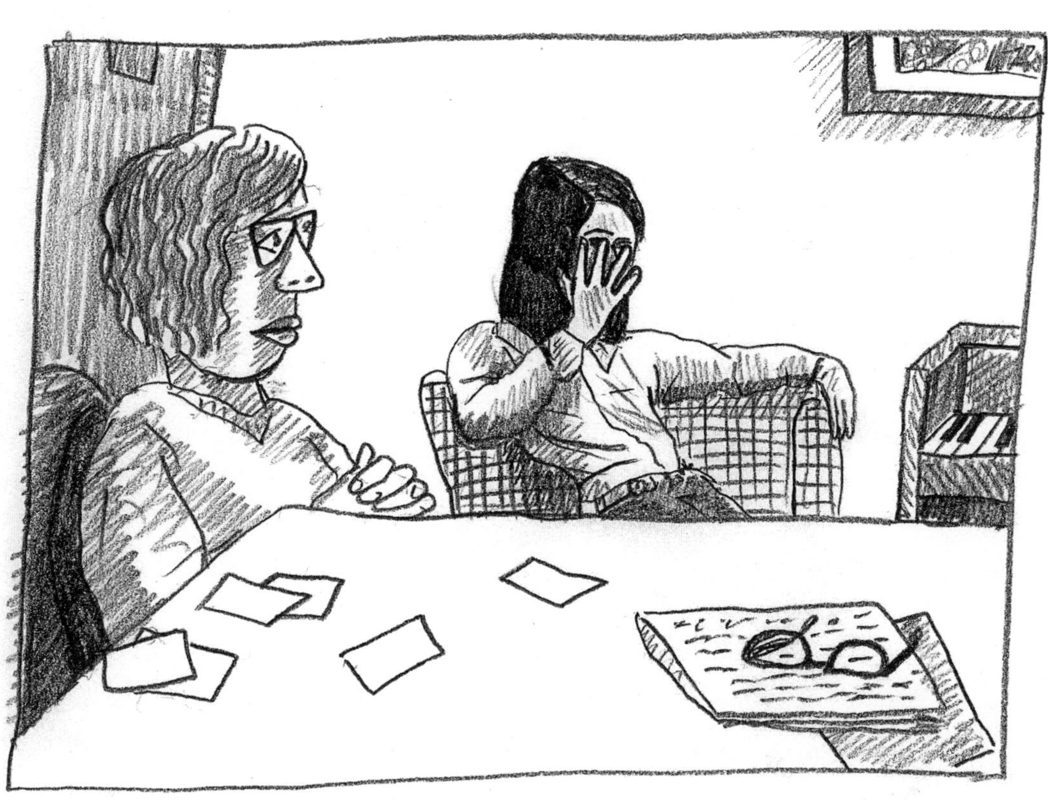

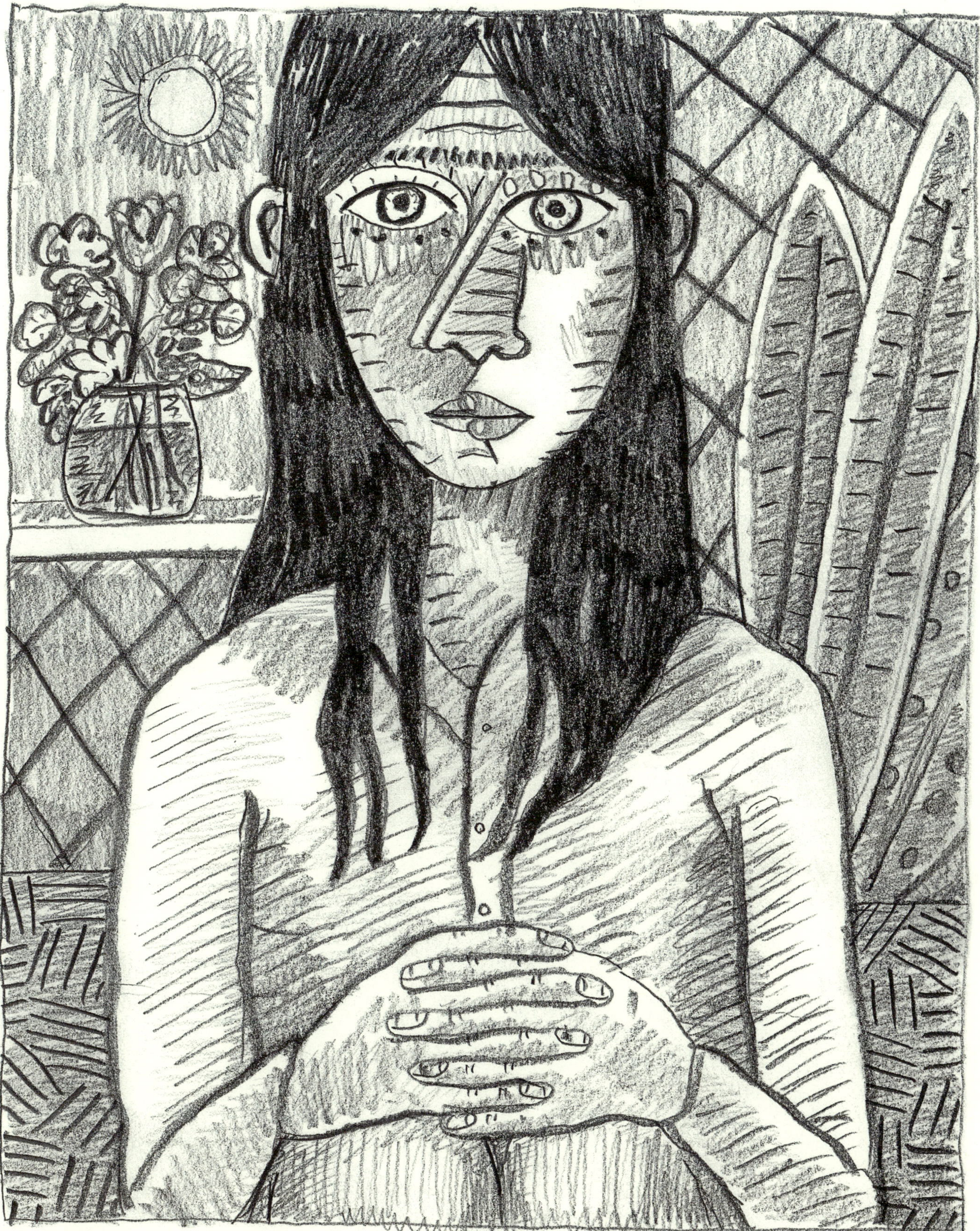

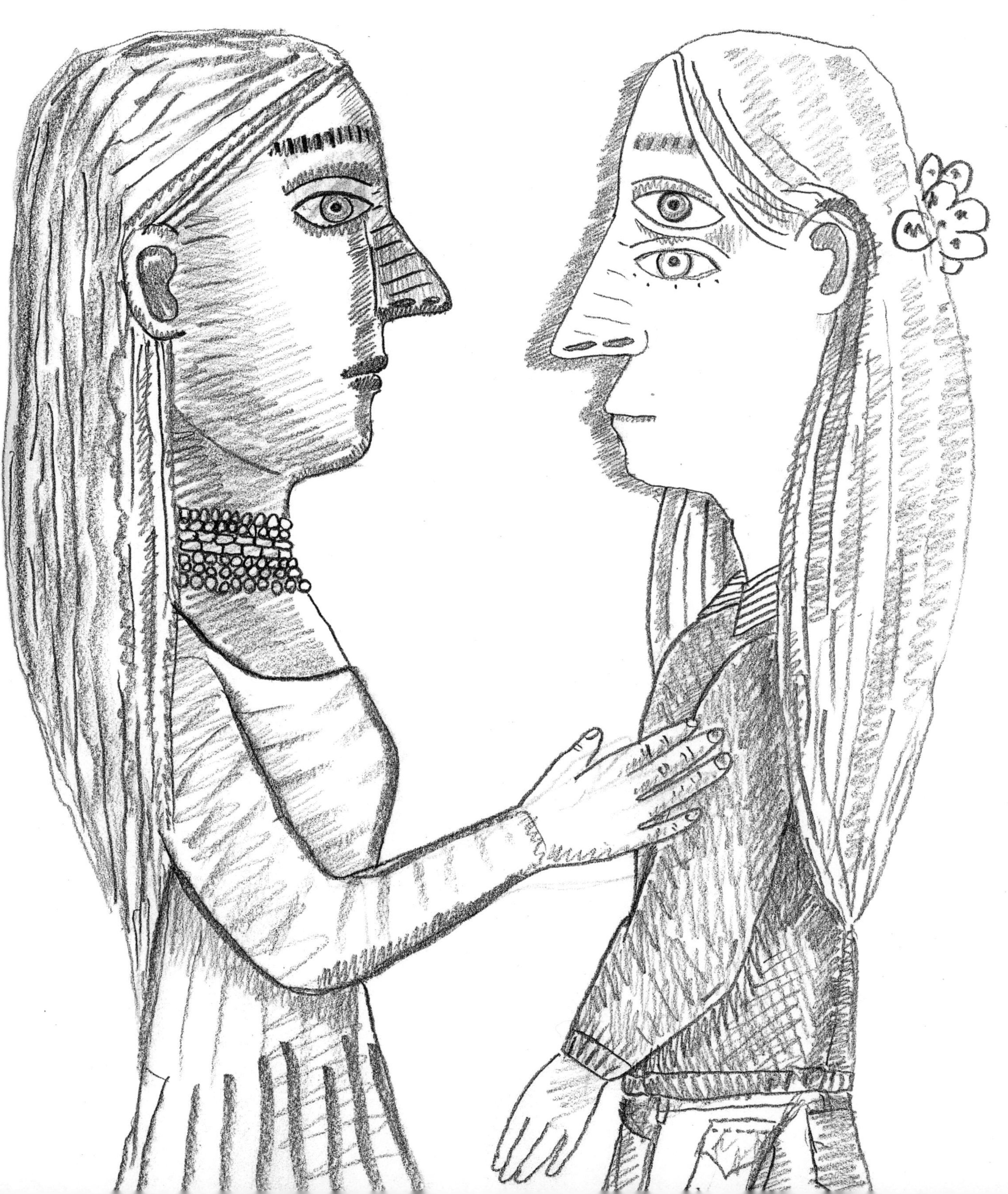

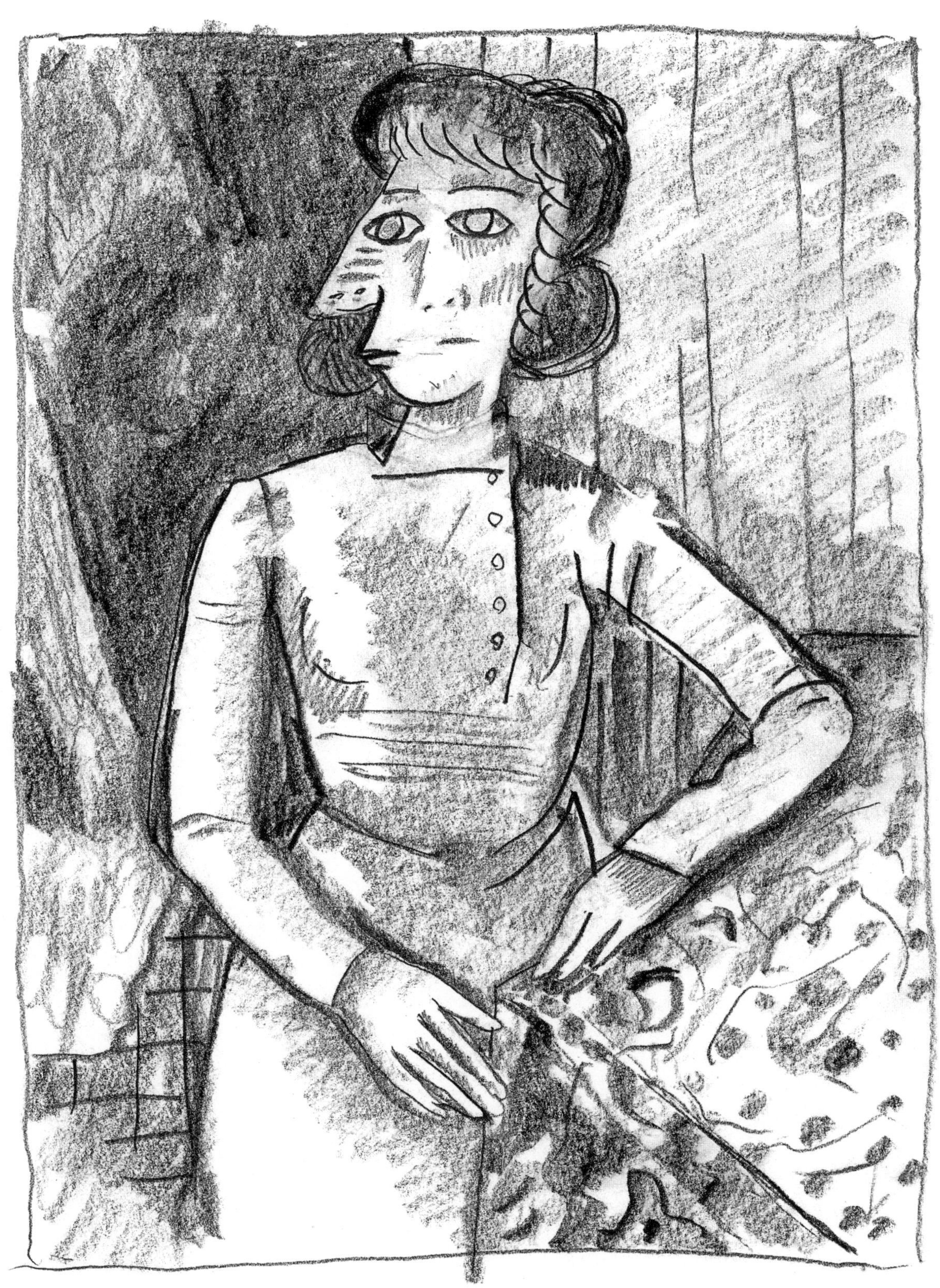

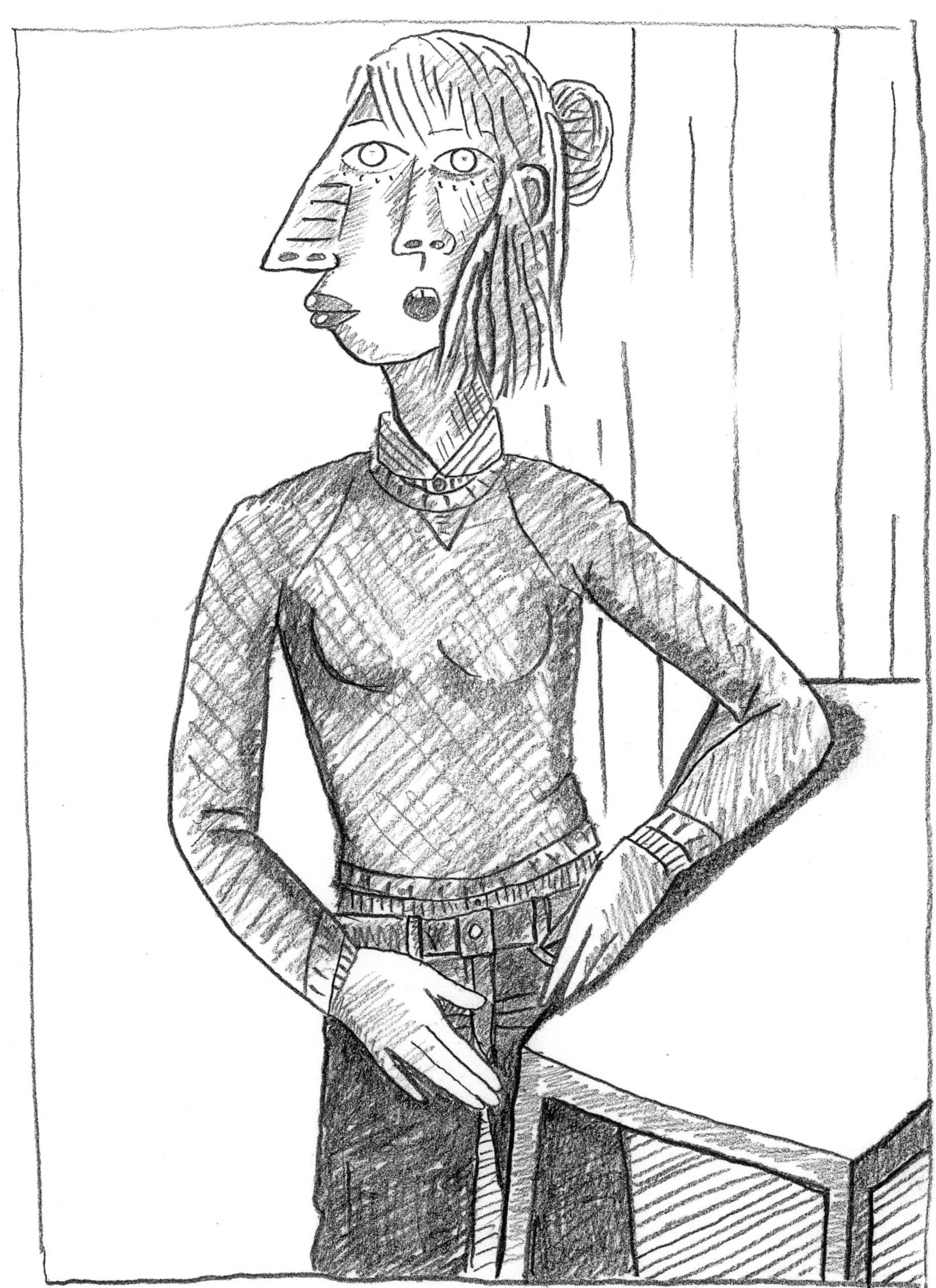

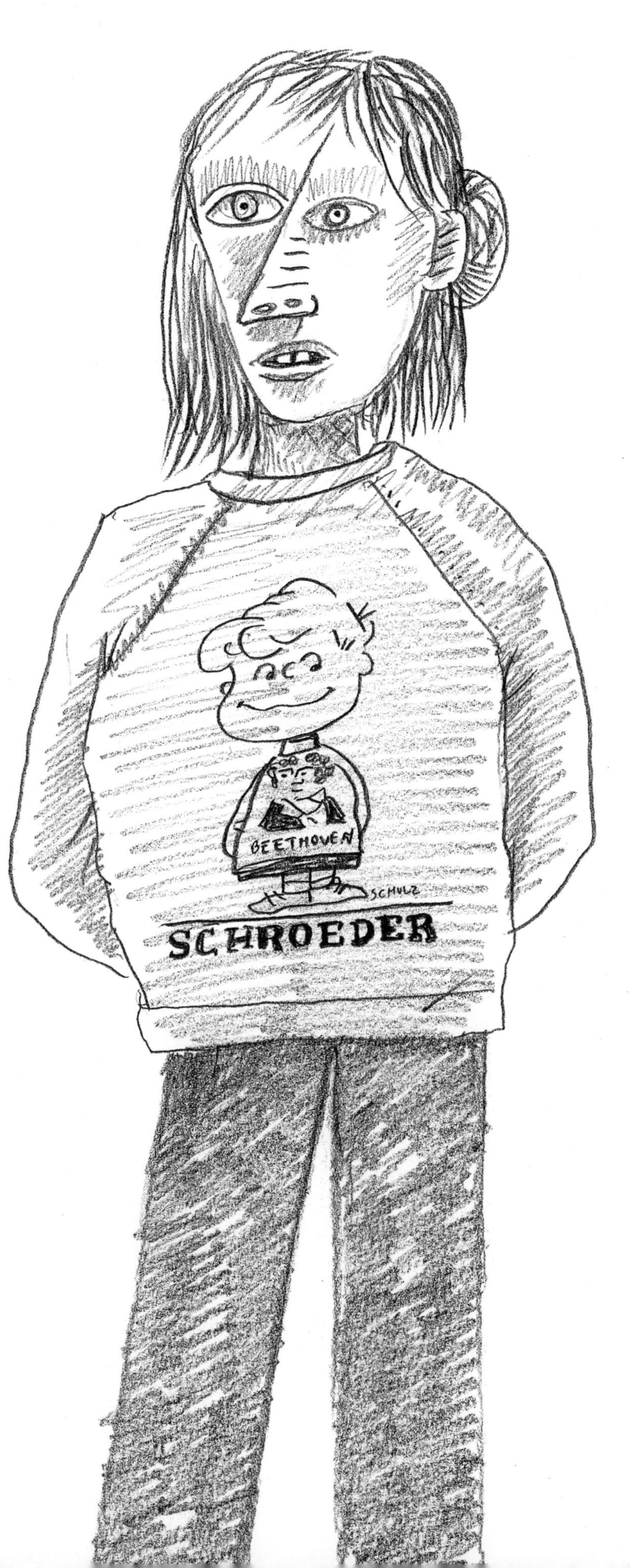

BEETHOVEN
SCHULZ
SCHROEDER

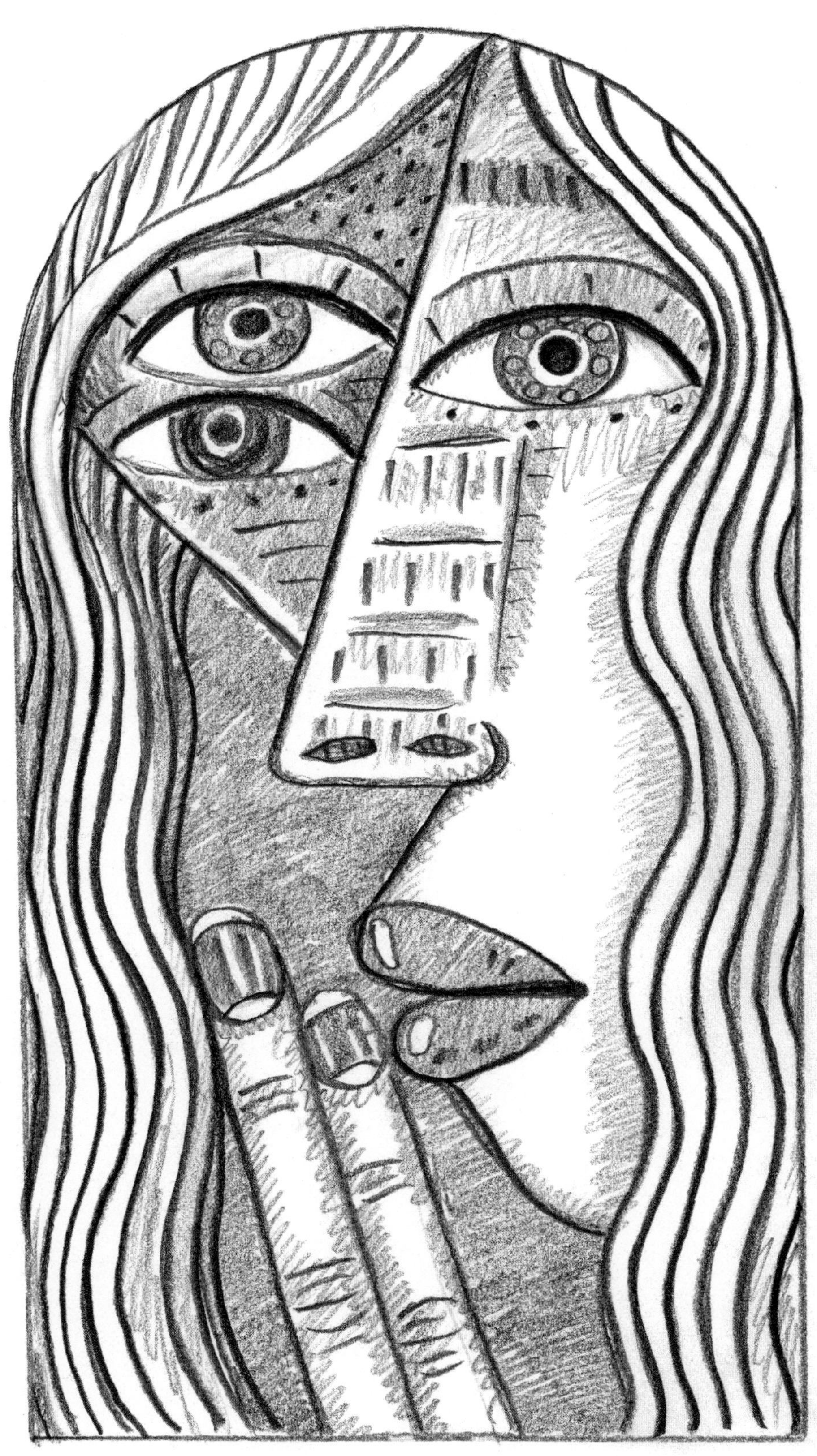

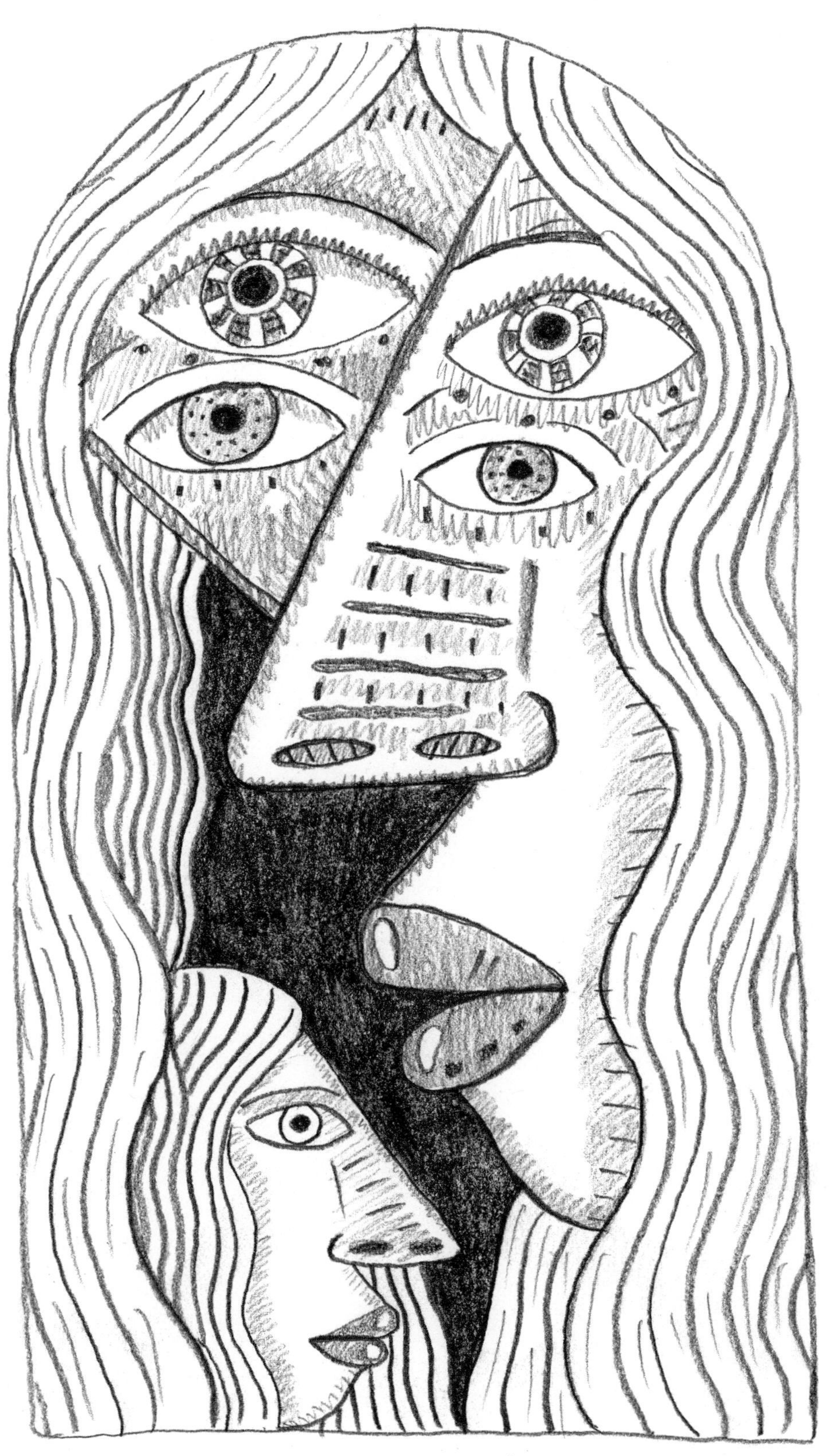

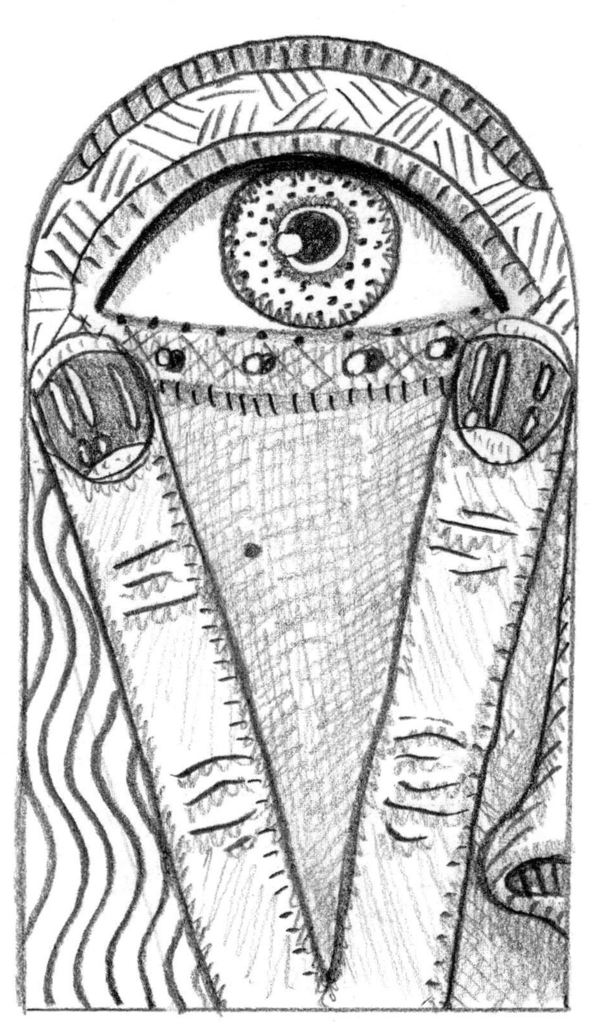

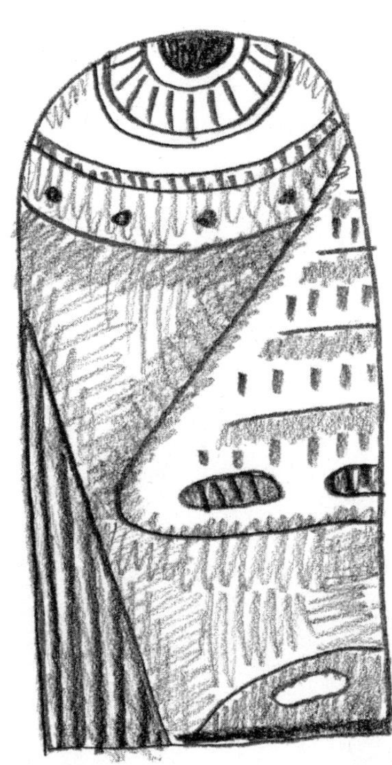

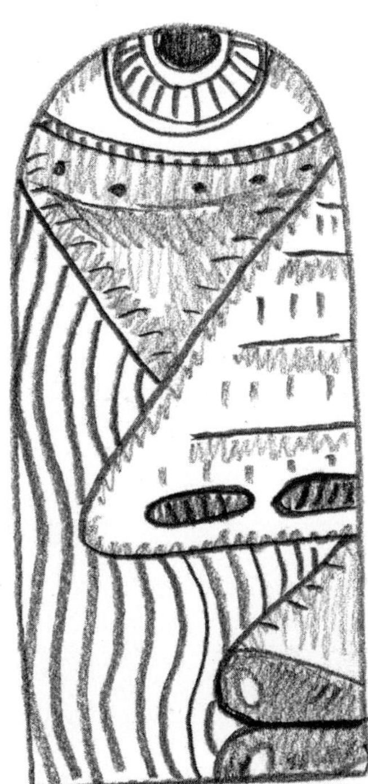

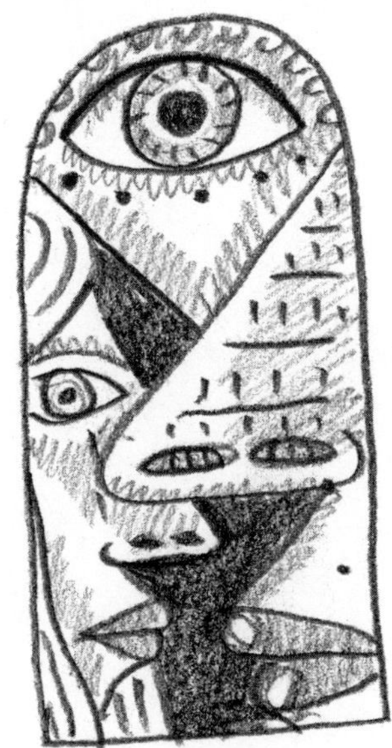

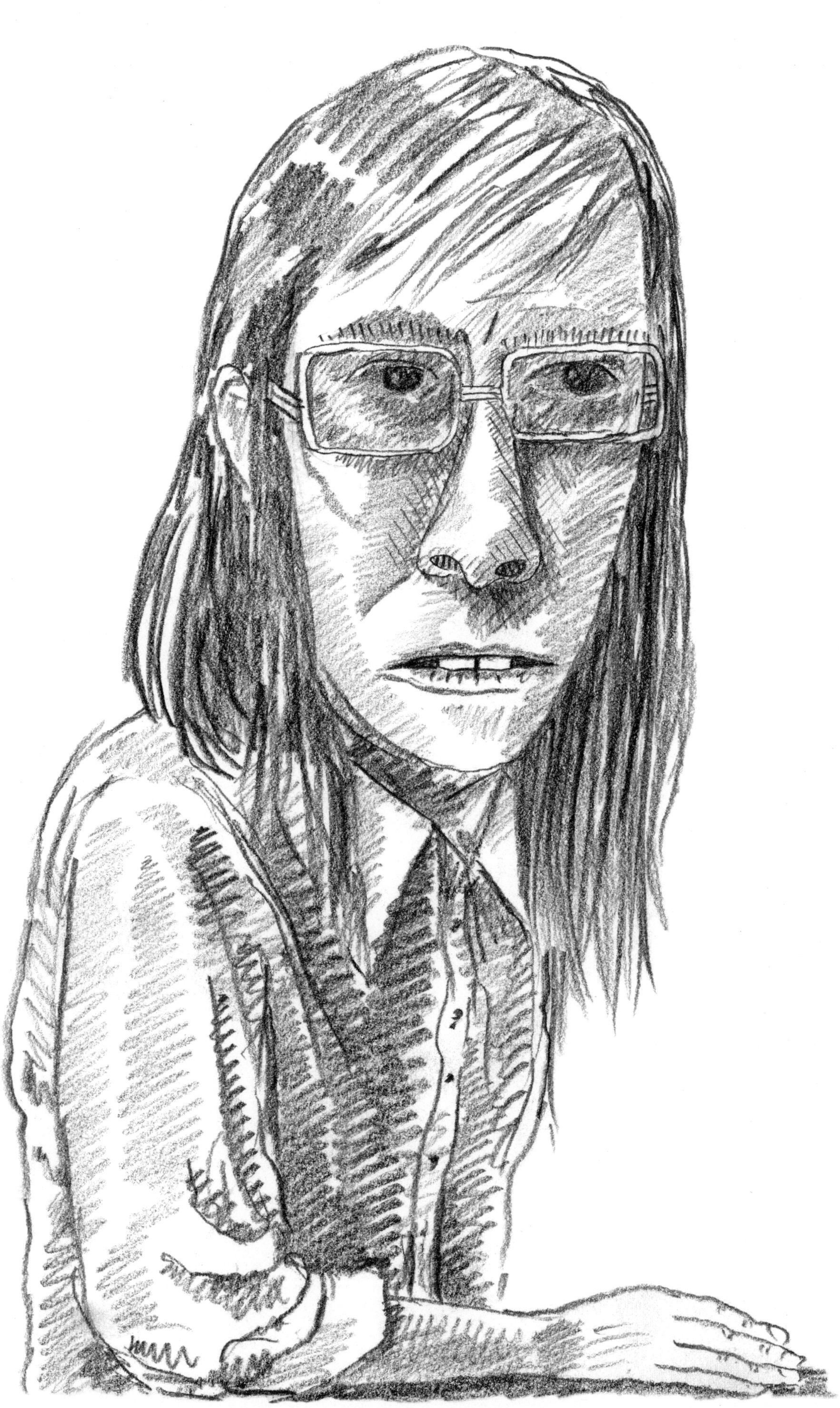
11-04-2022

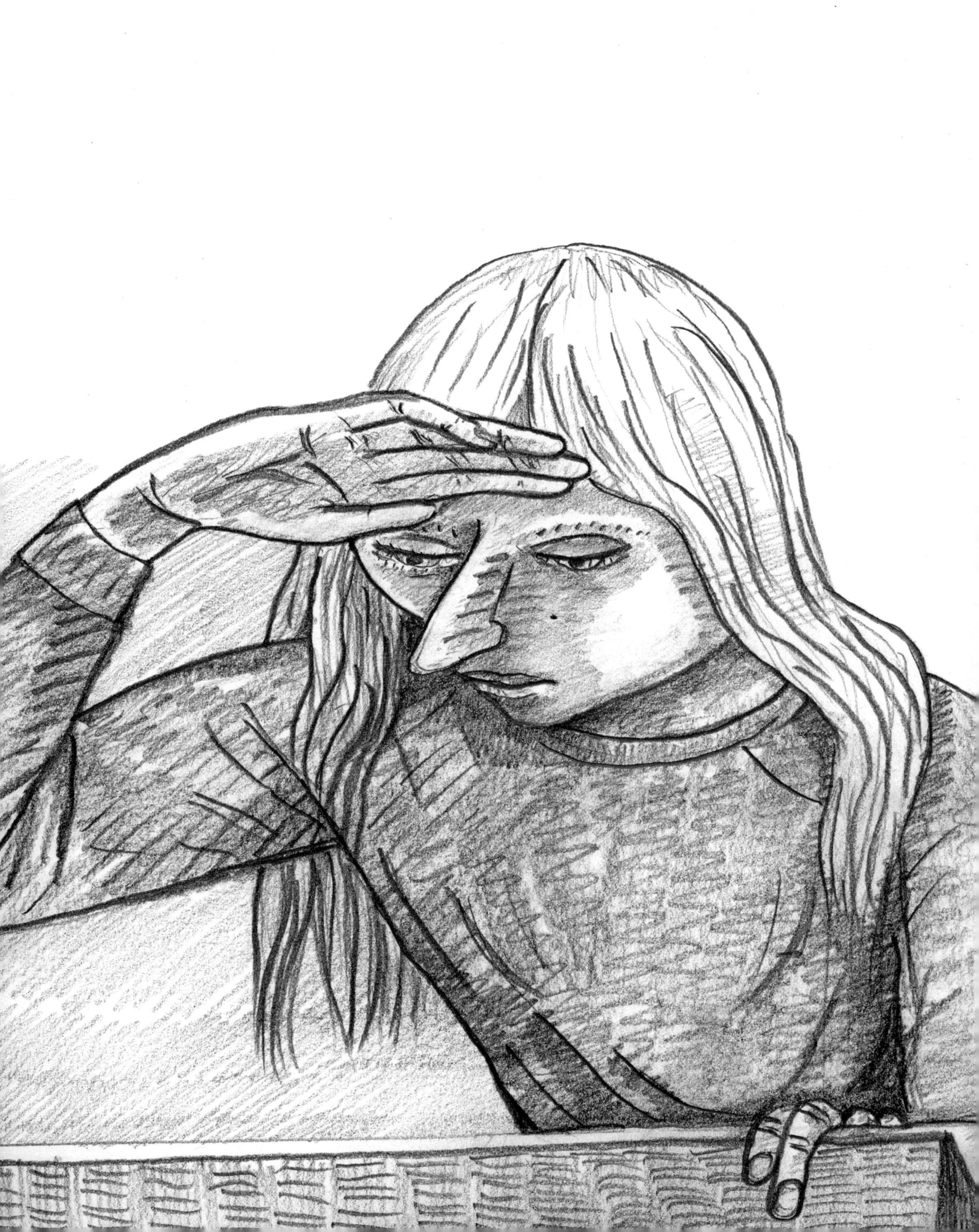

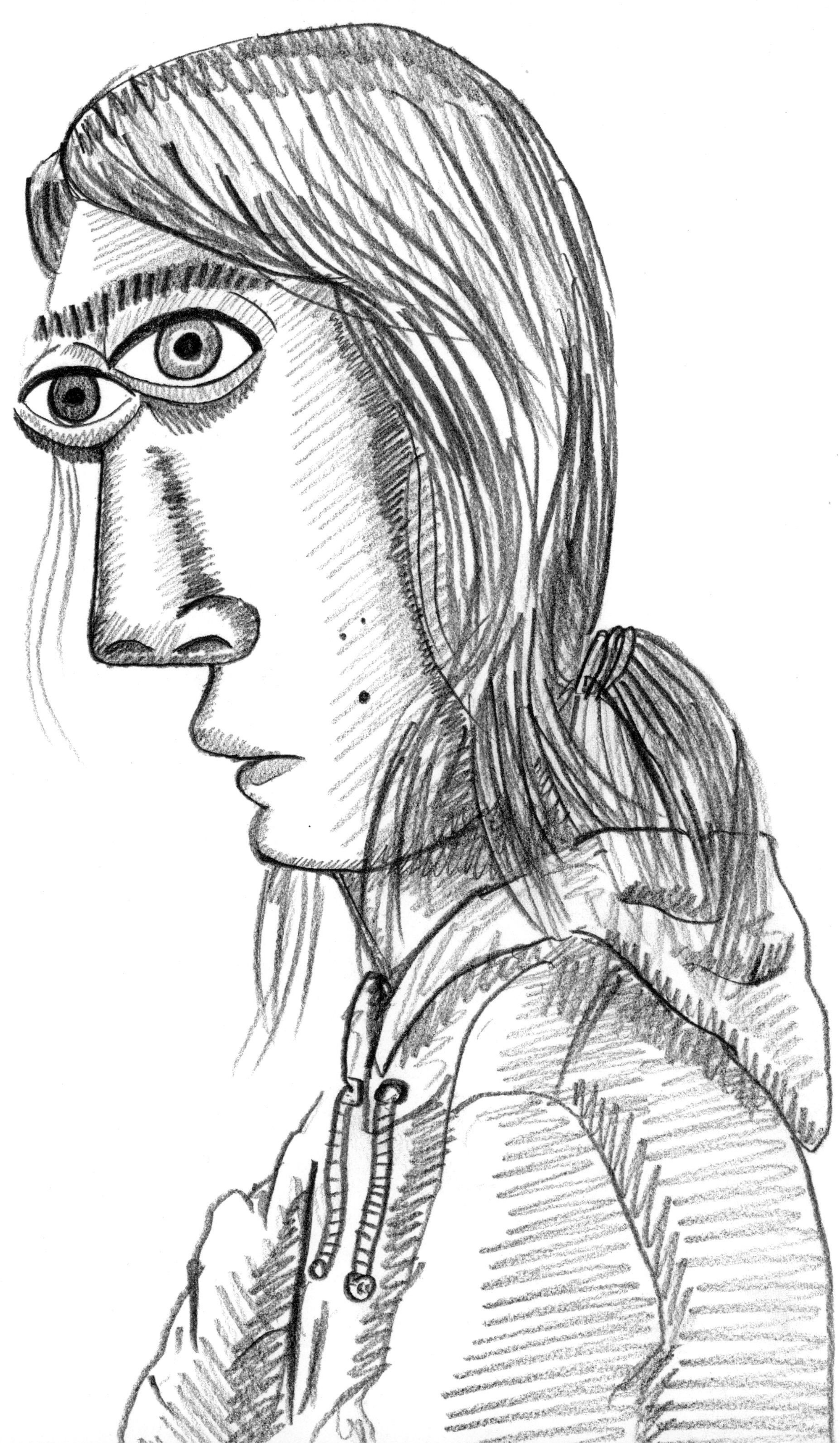

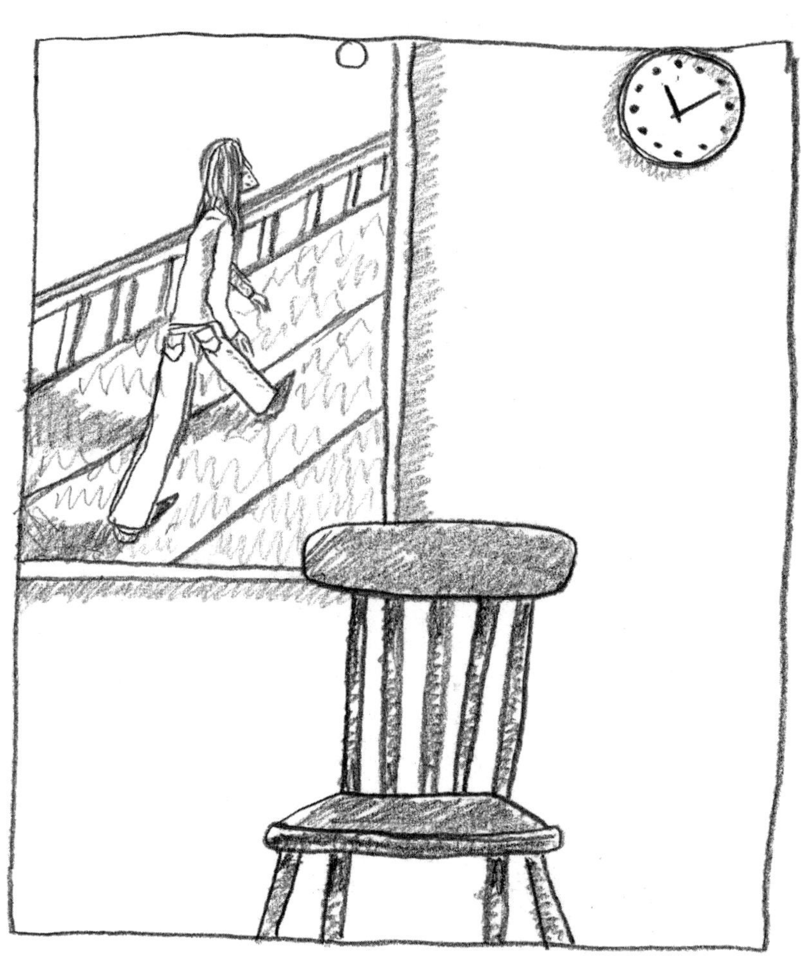

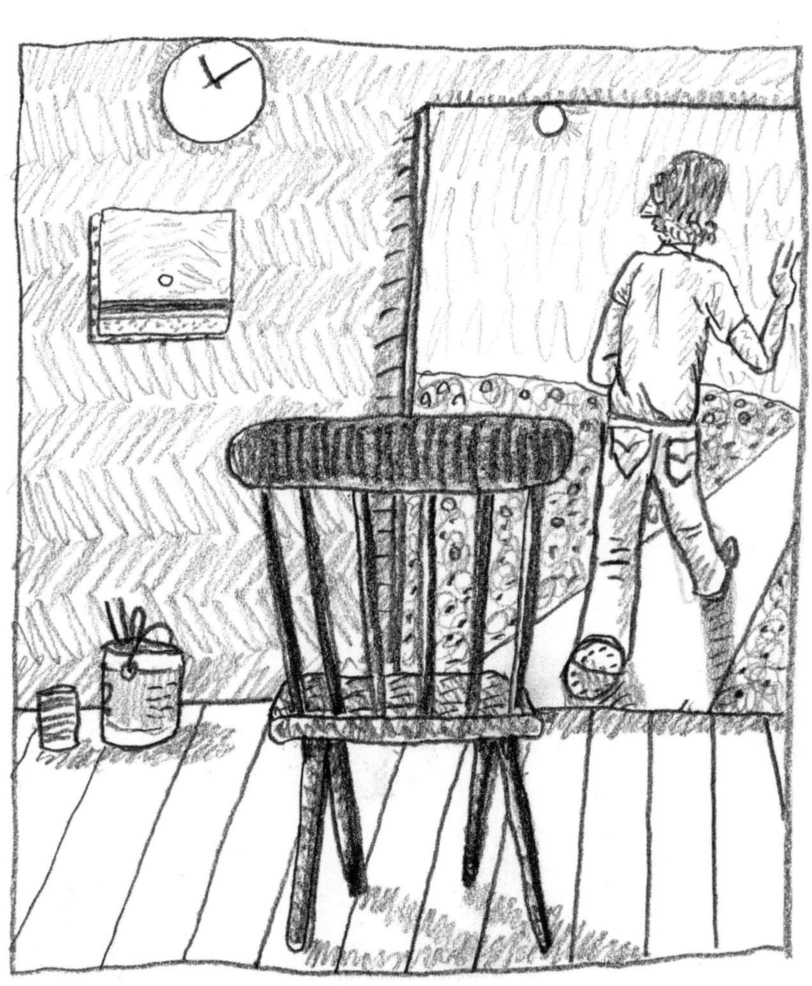

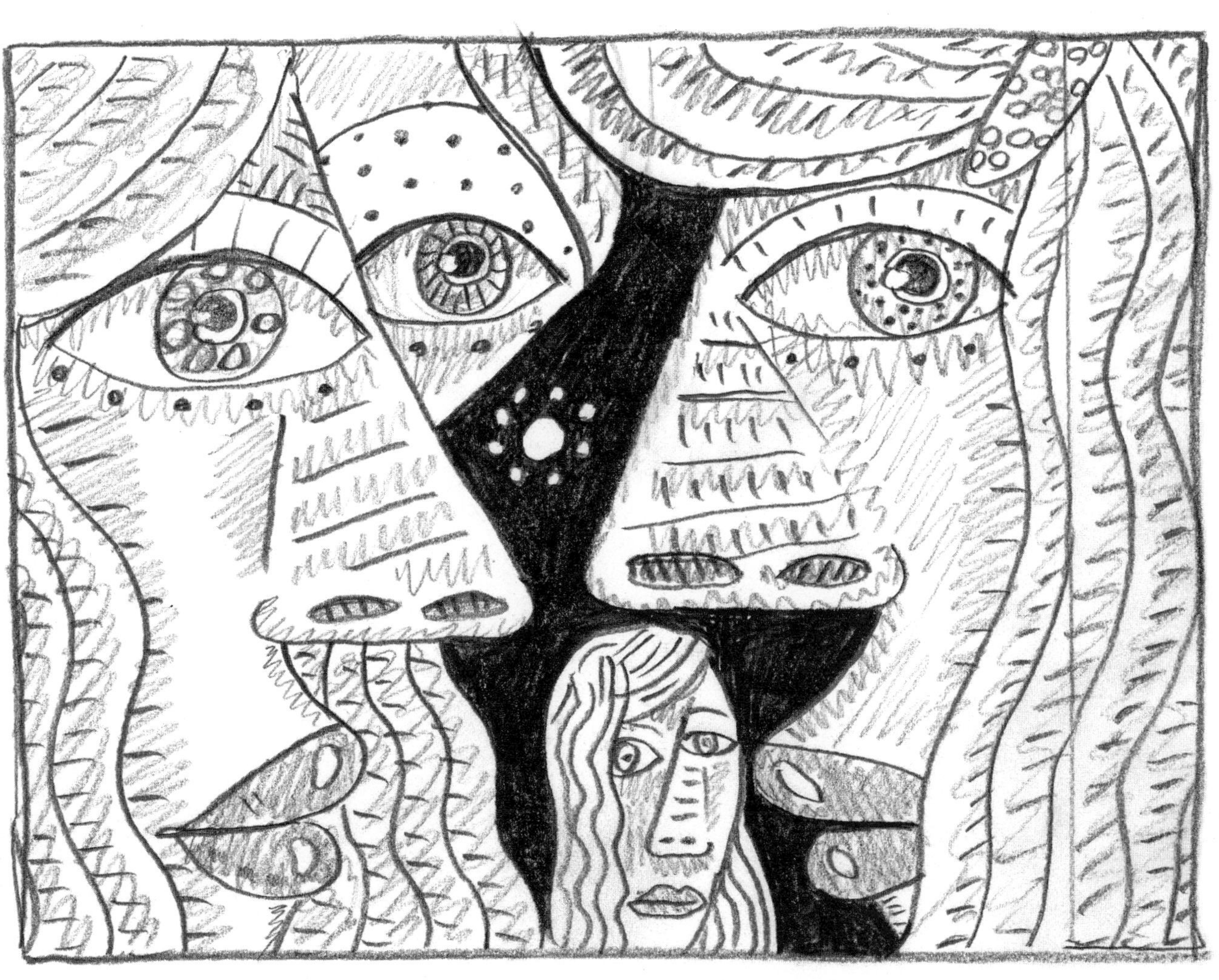

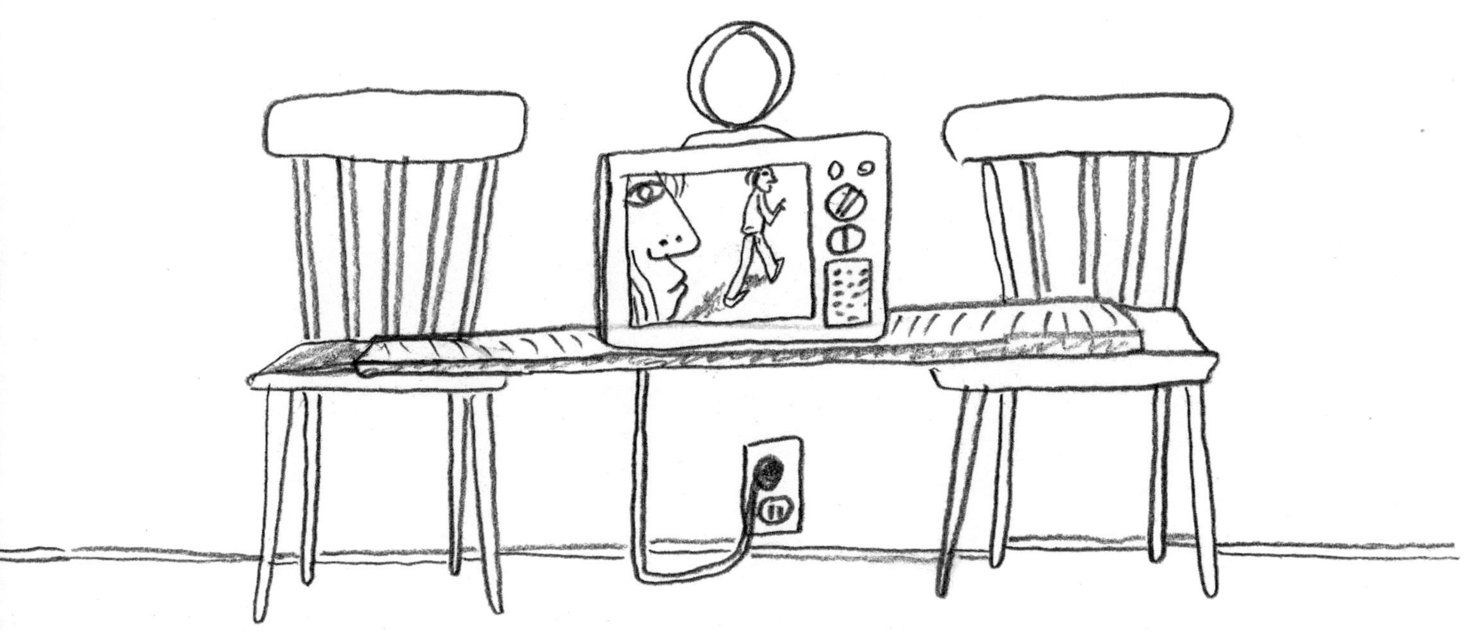

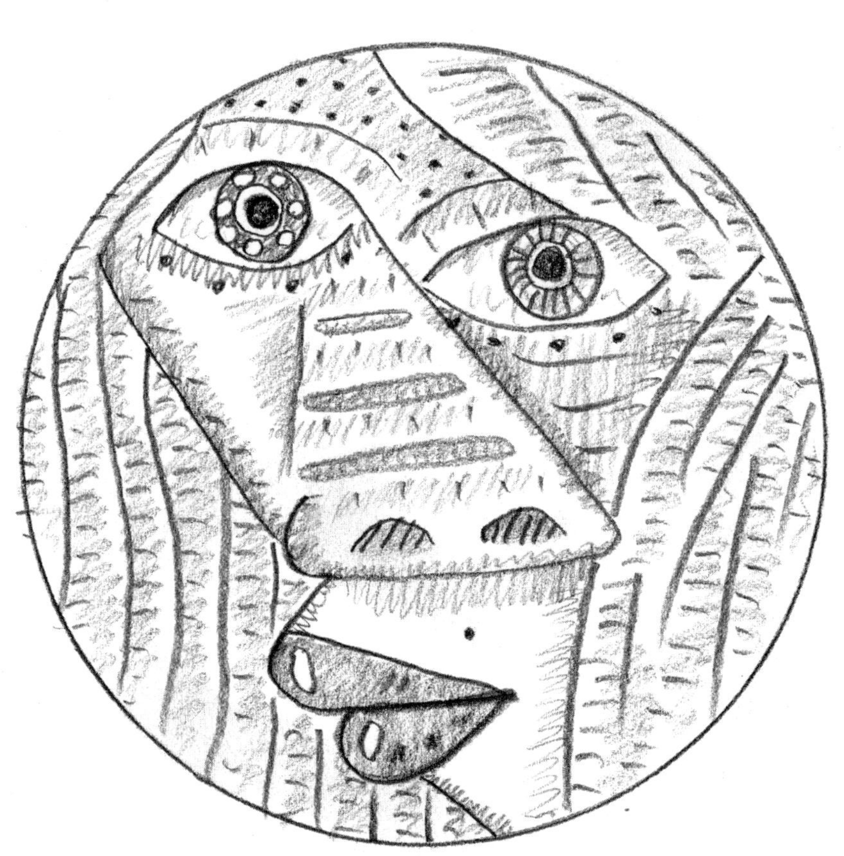

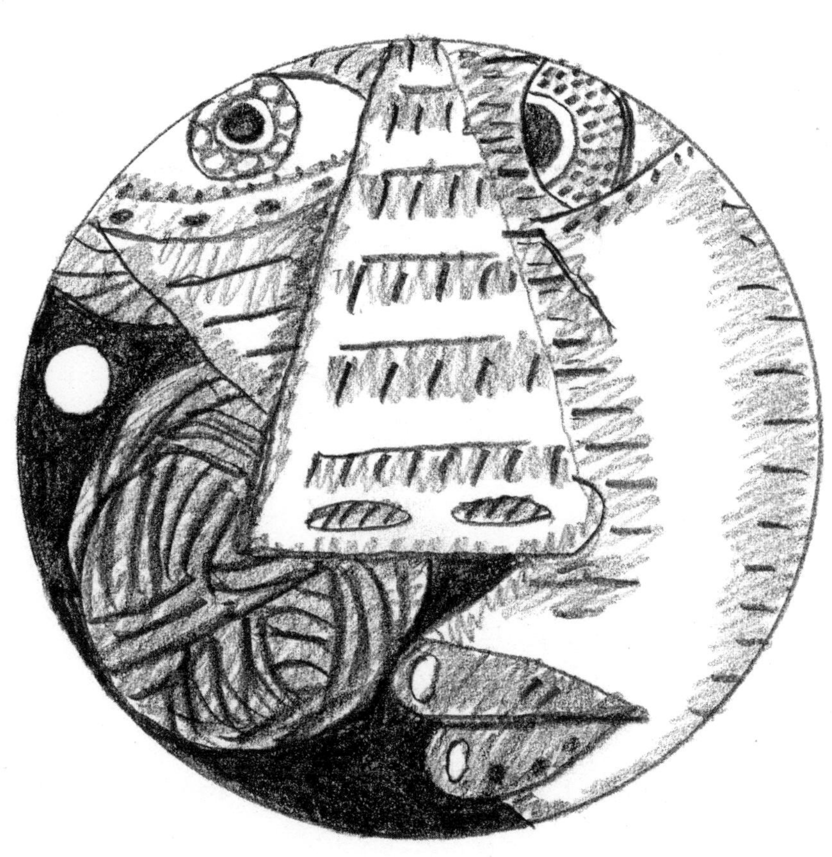

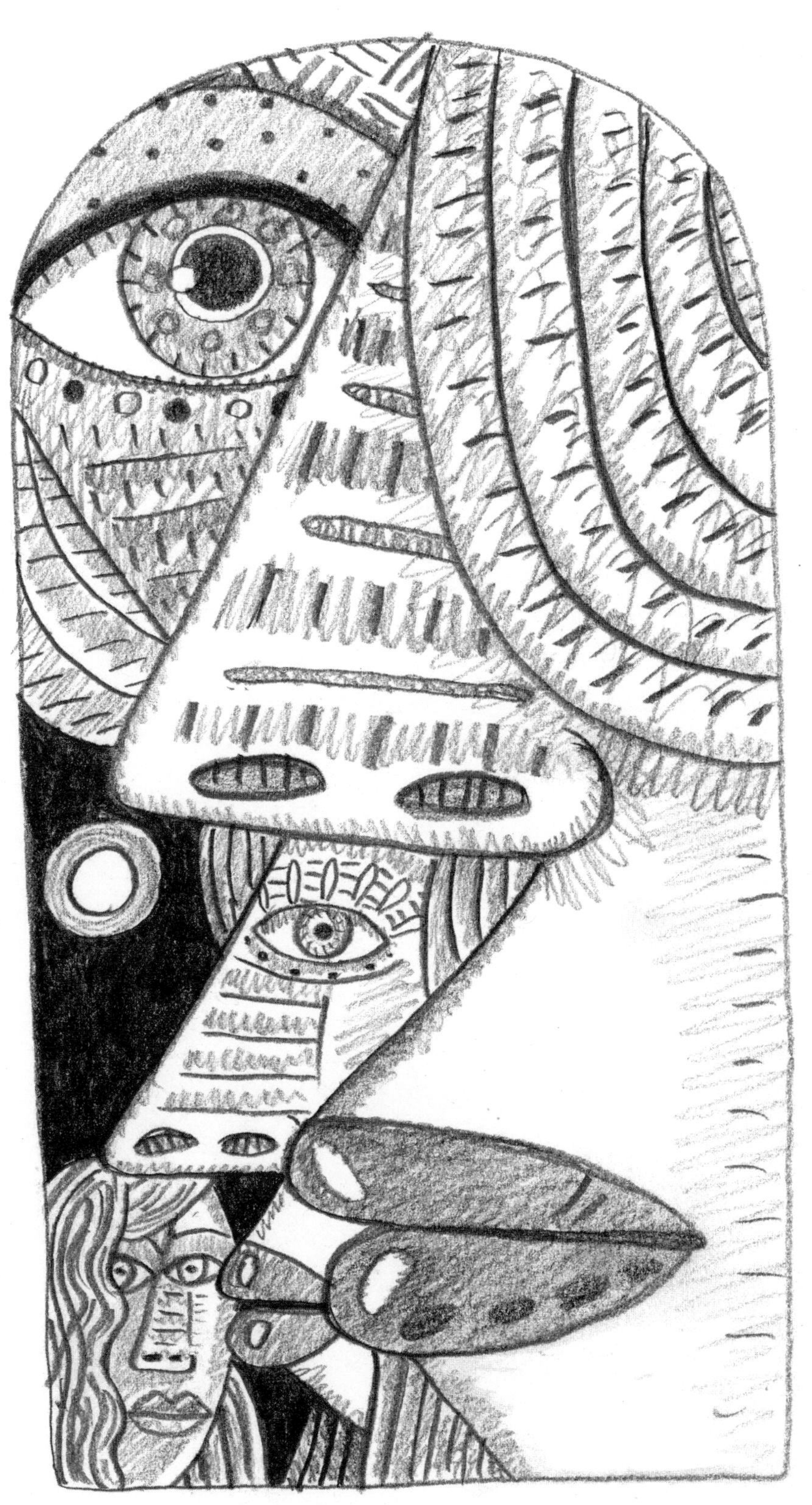

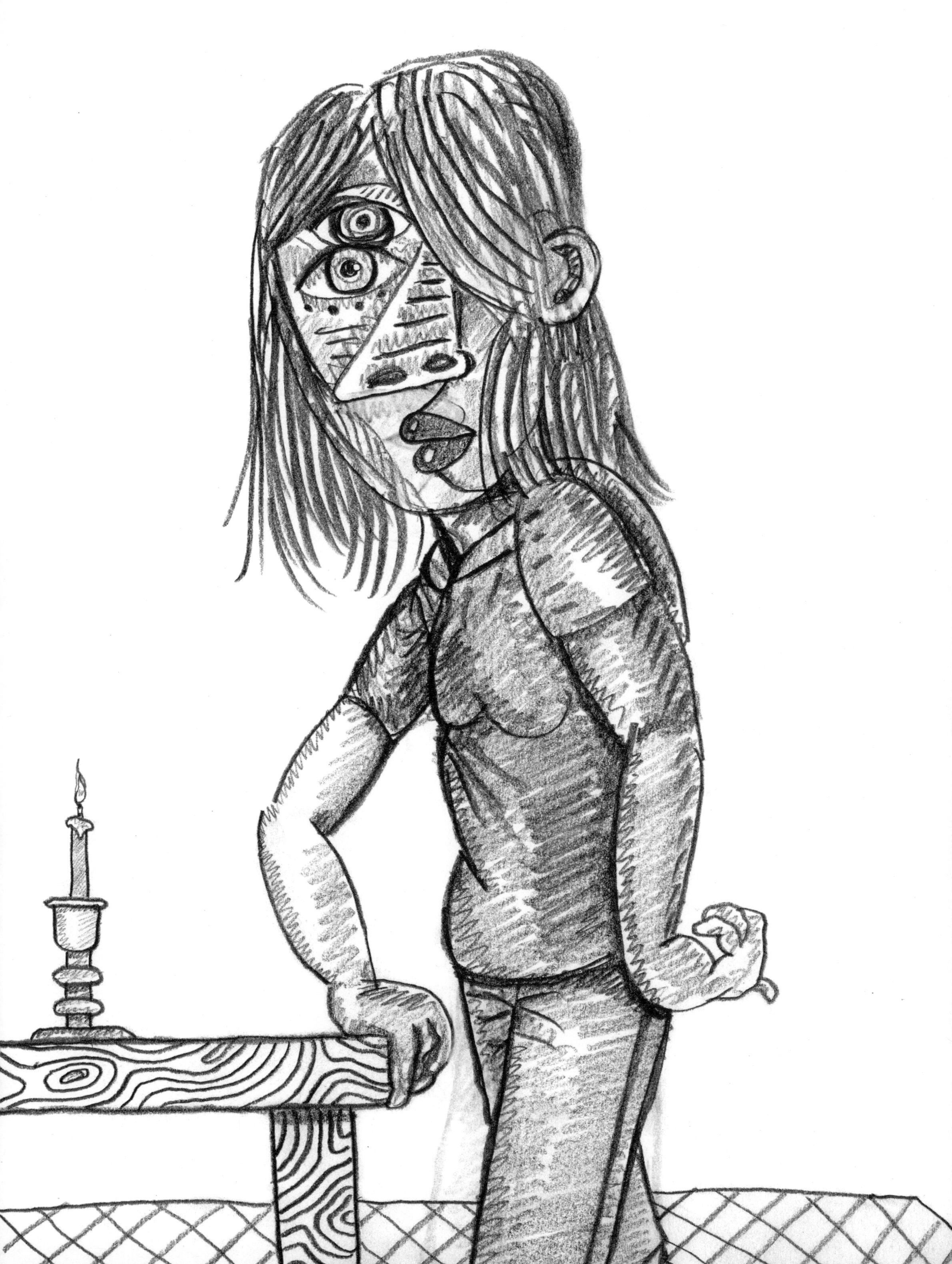

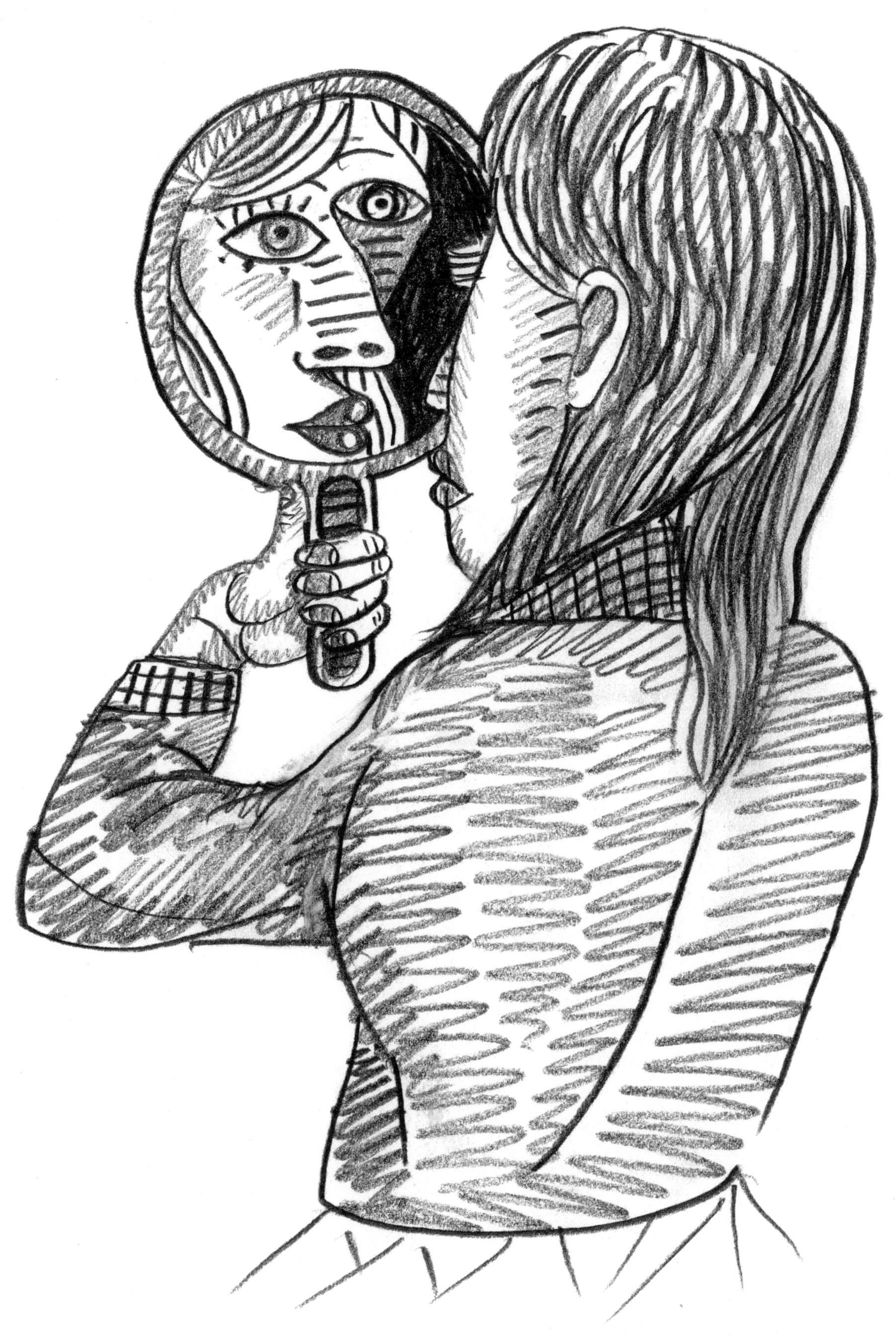

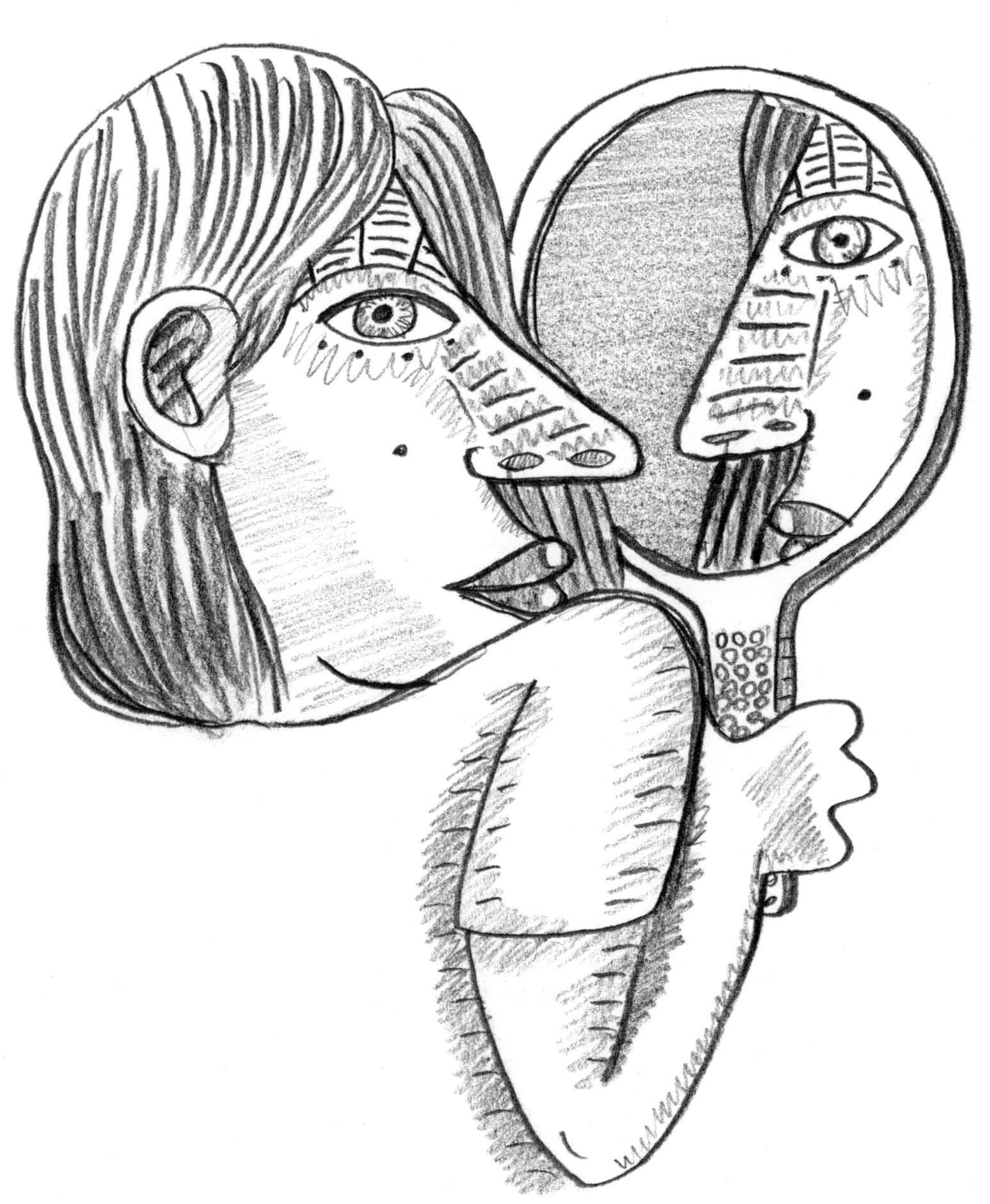

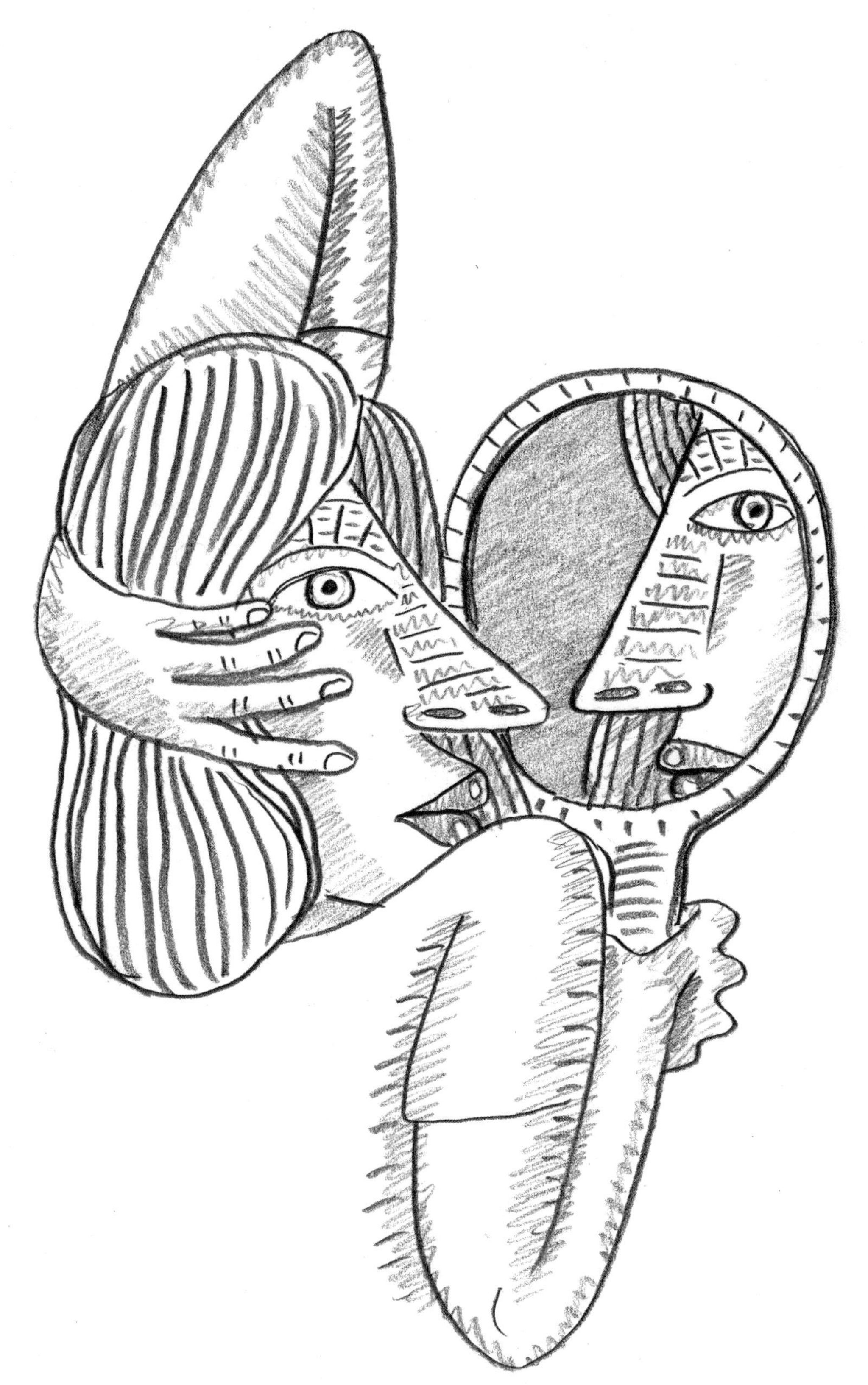

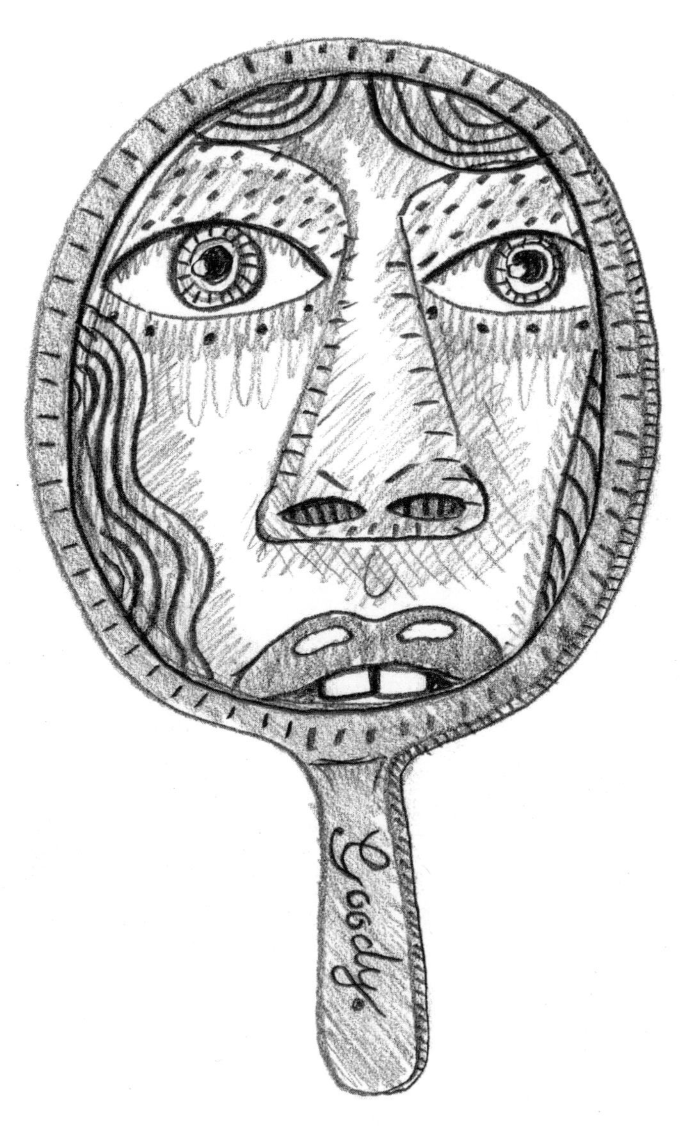
Goody.

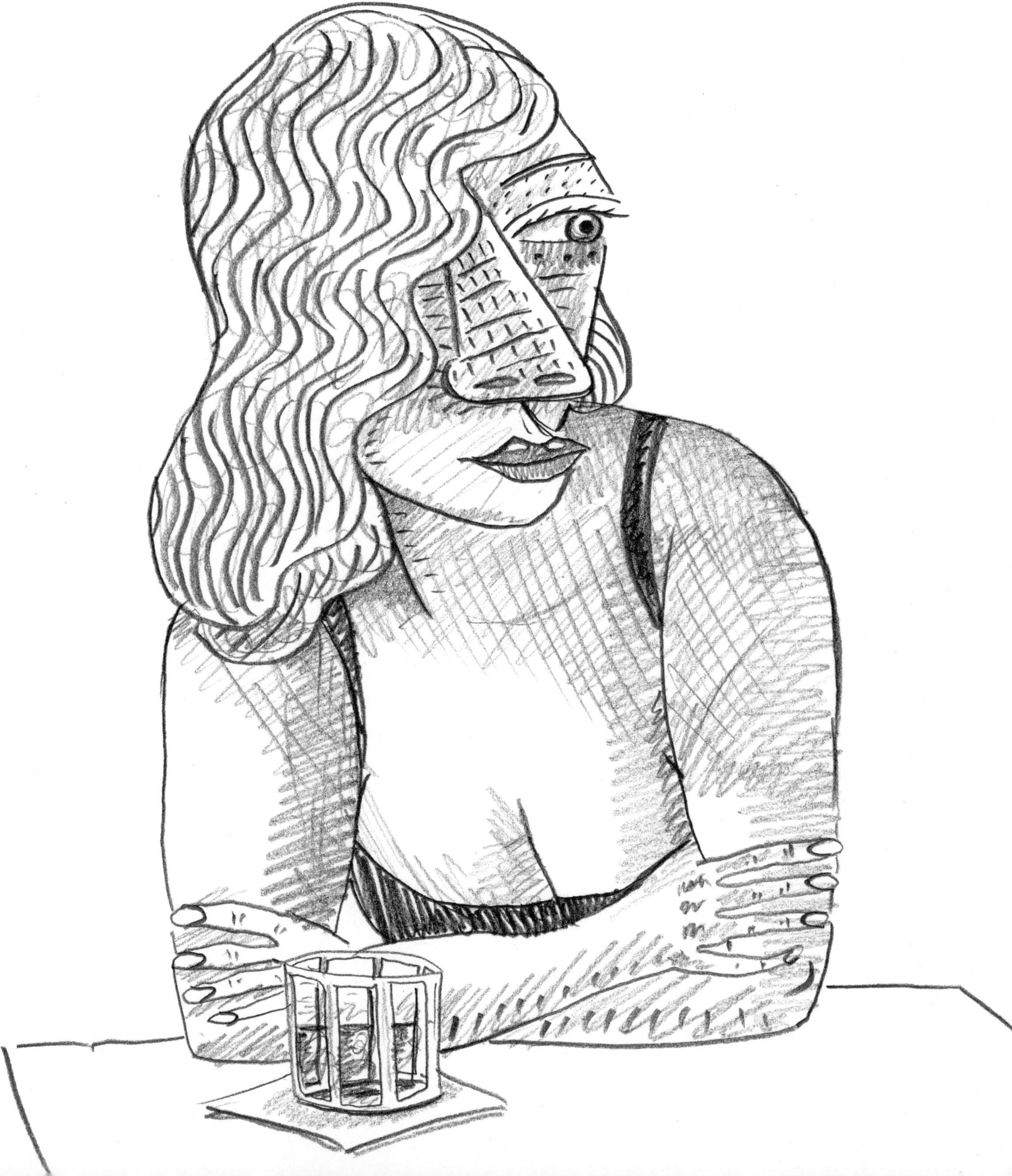

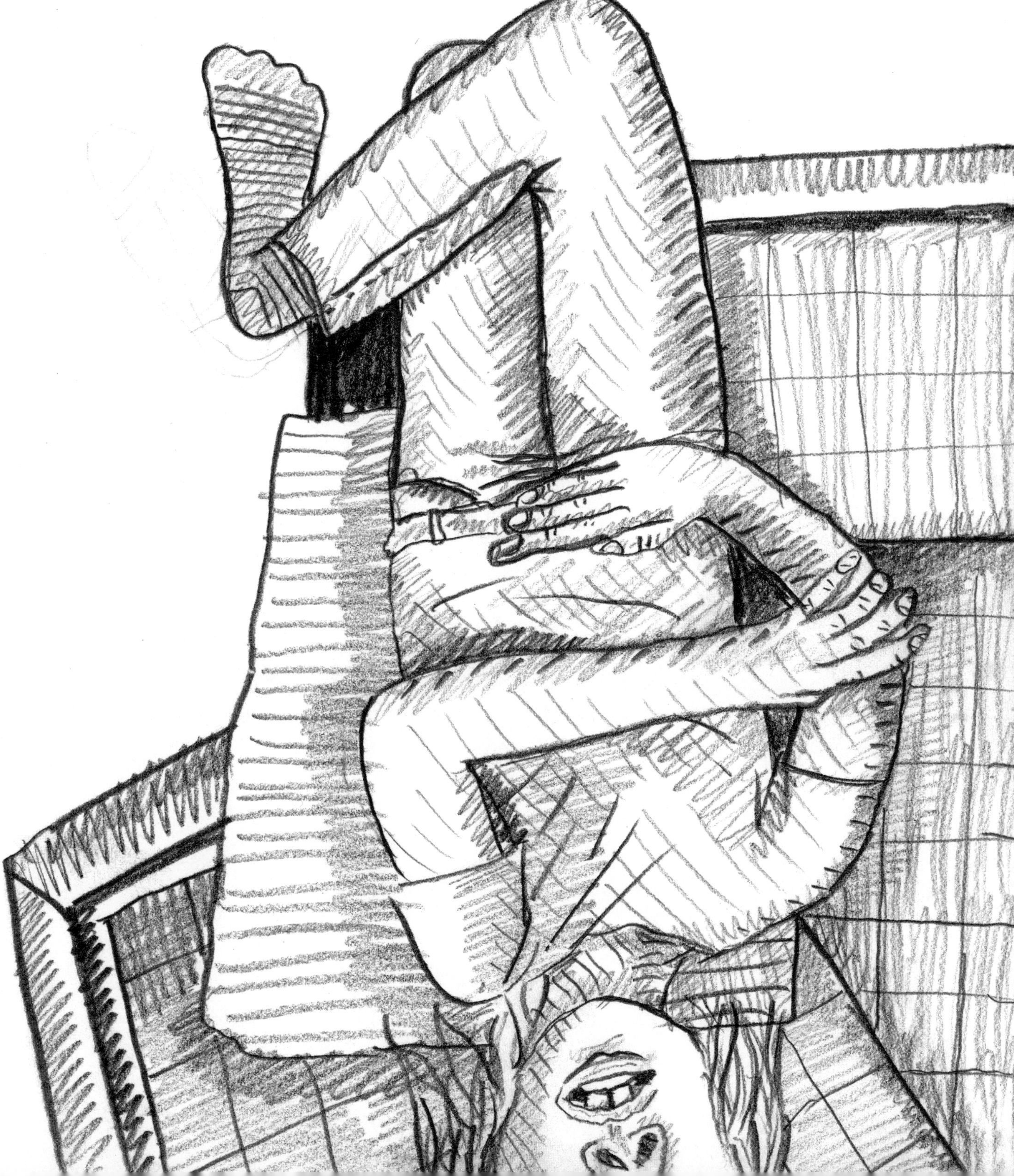

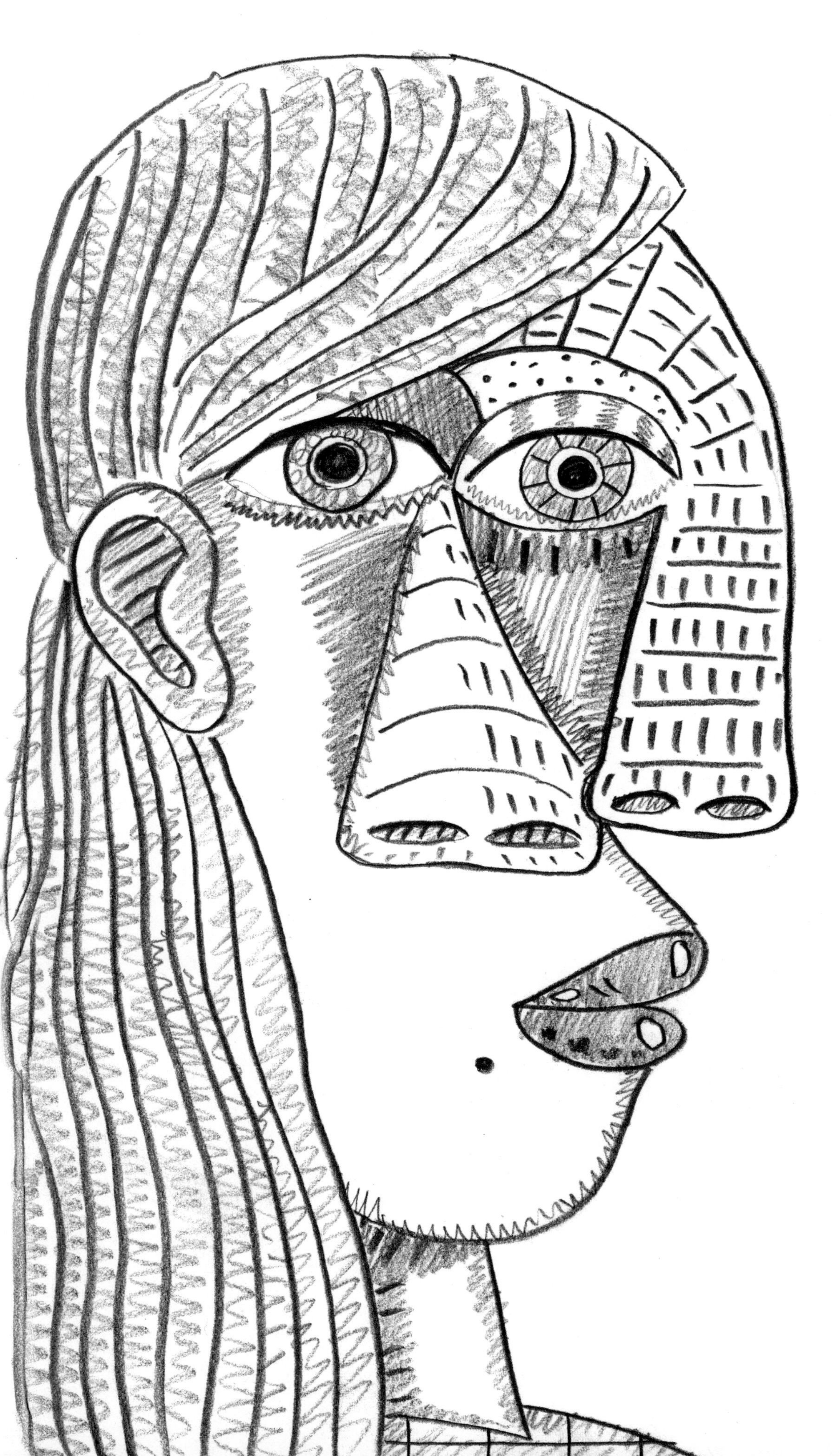

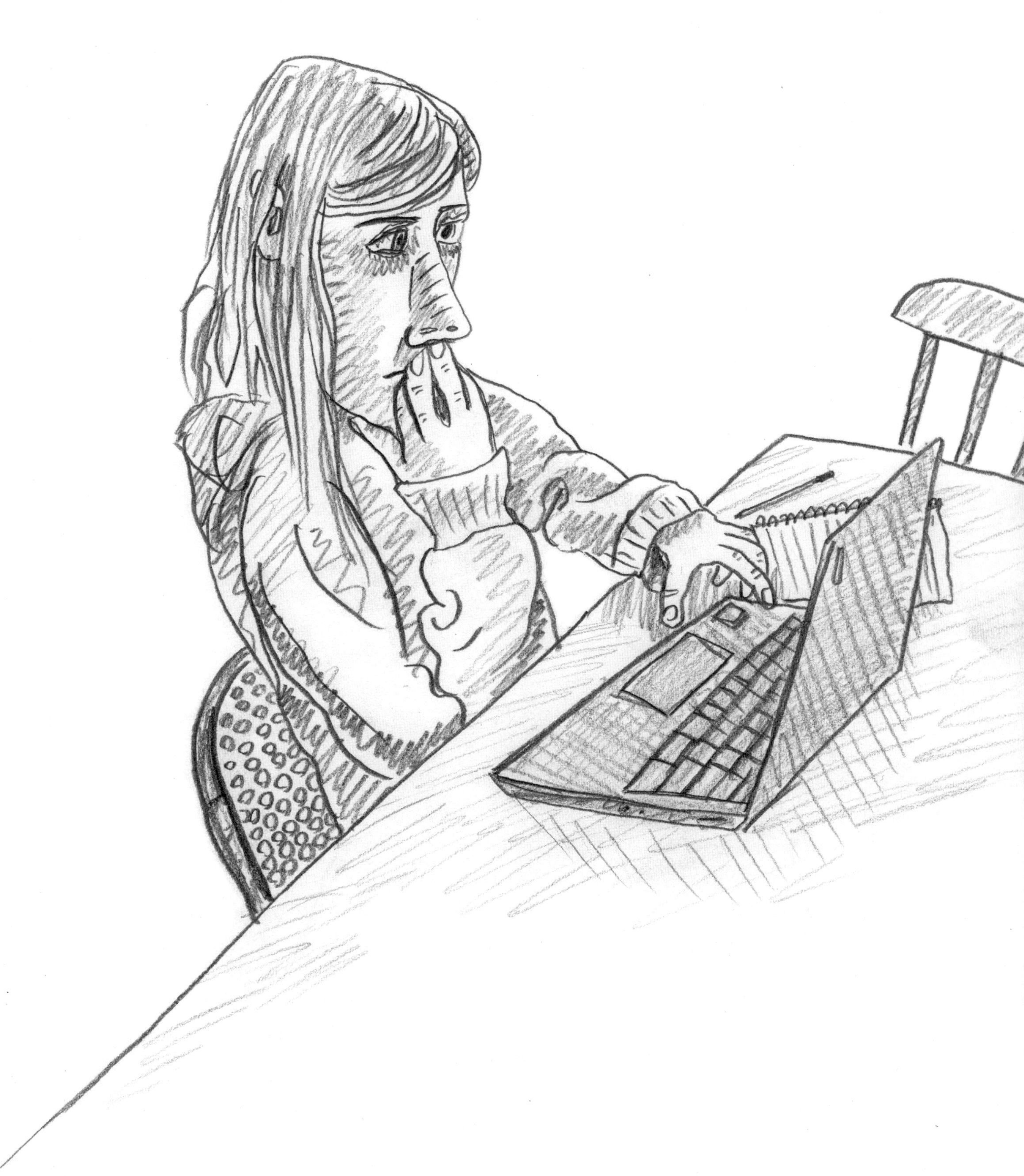

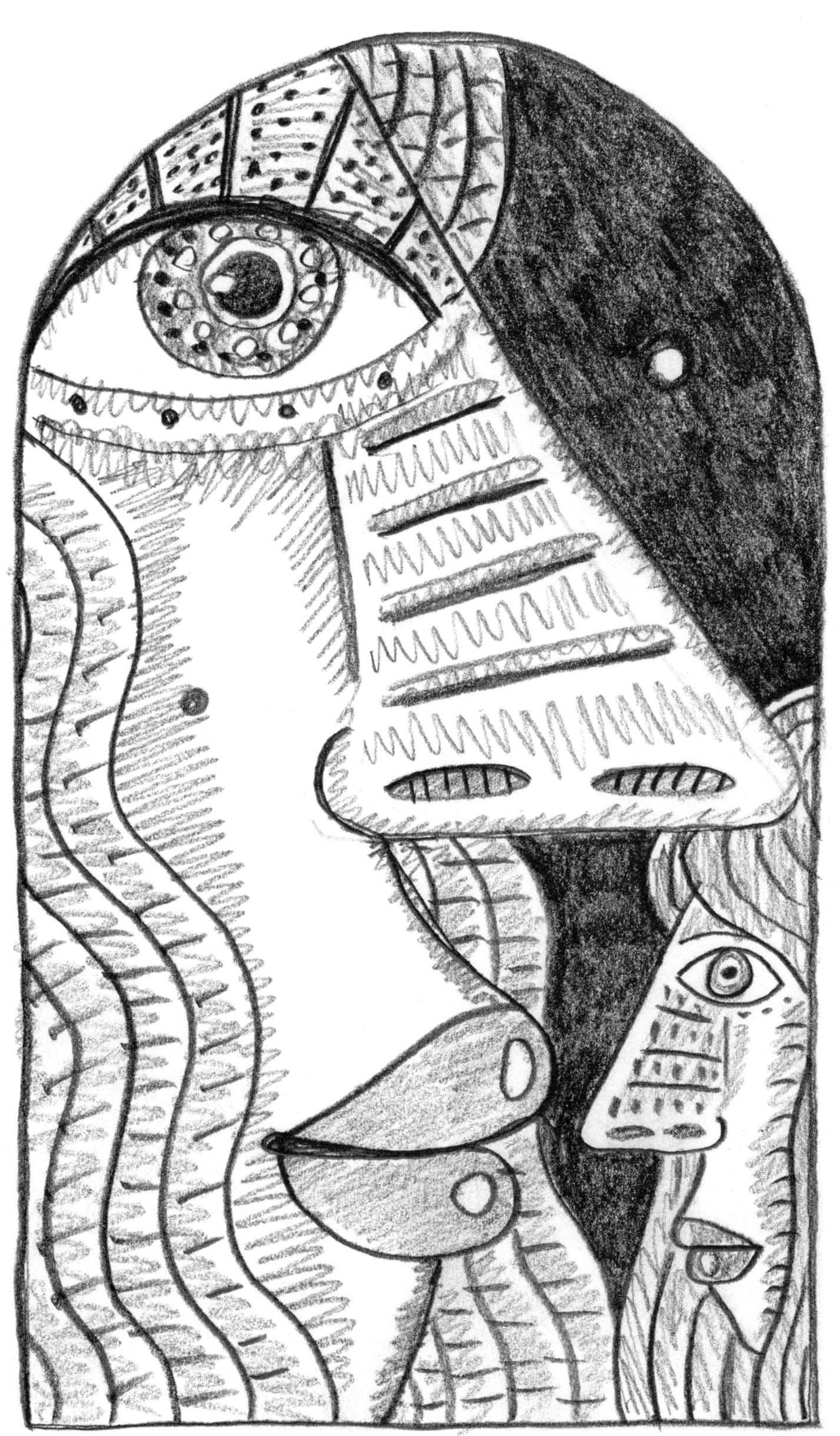

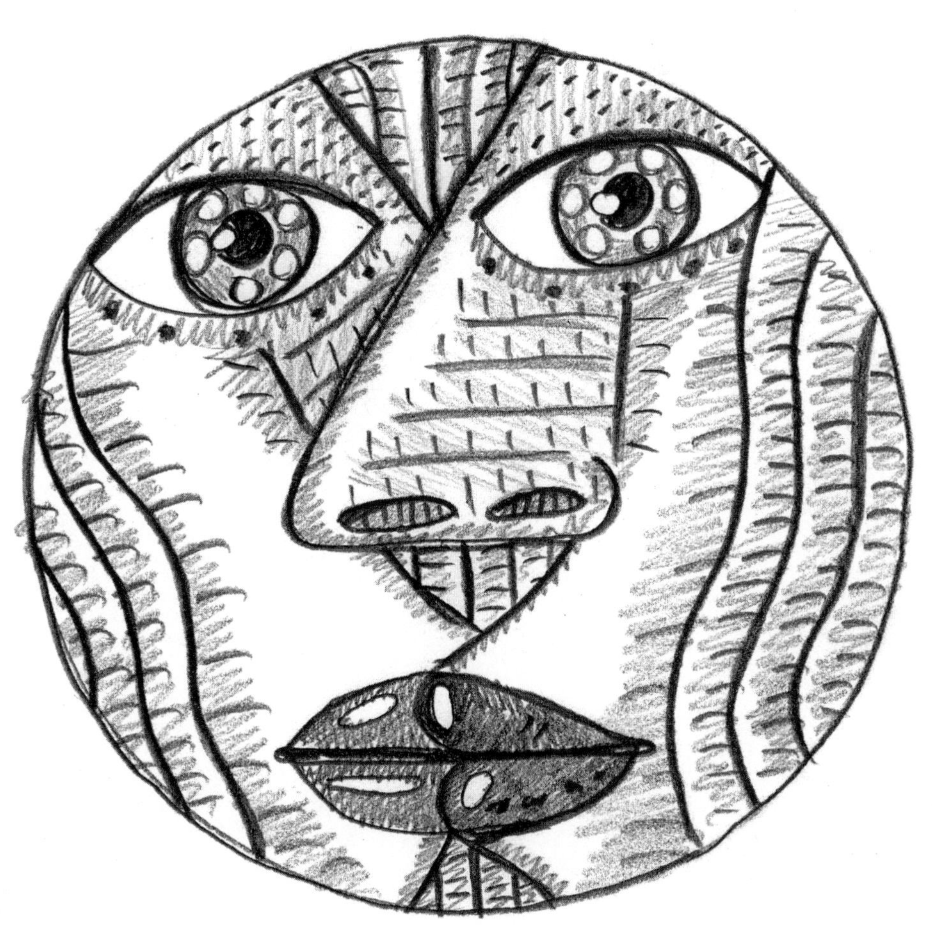

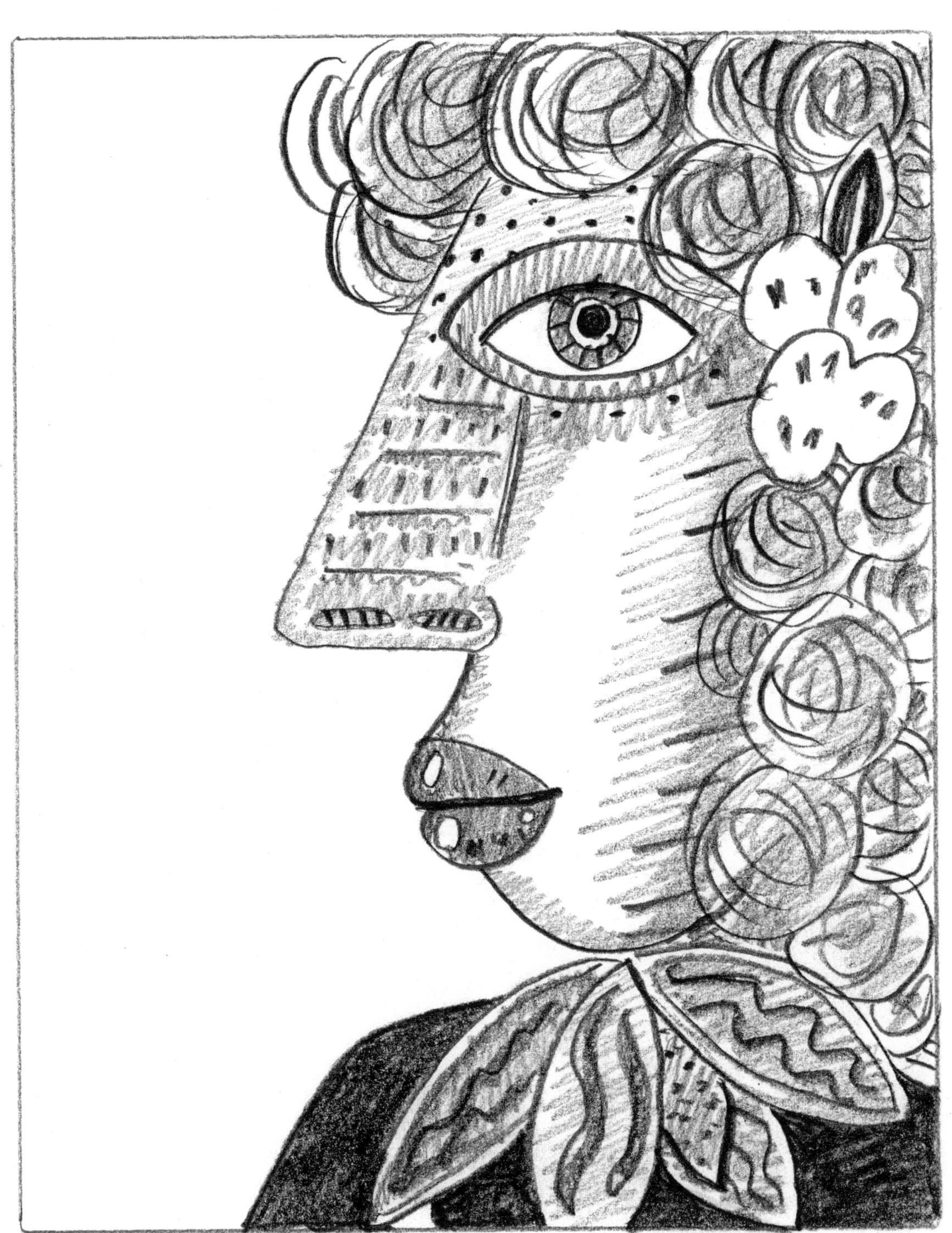

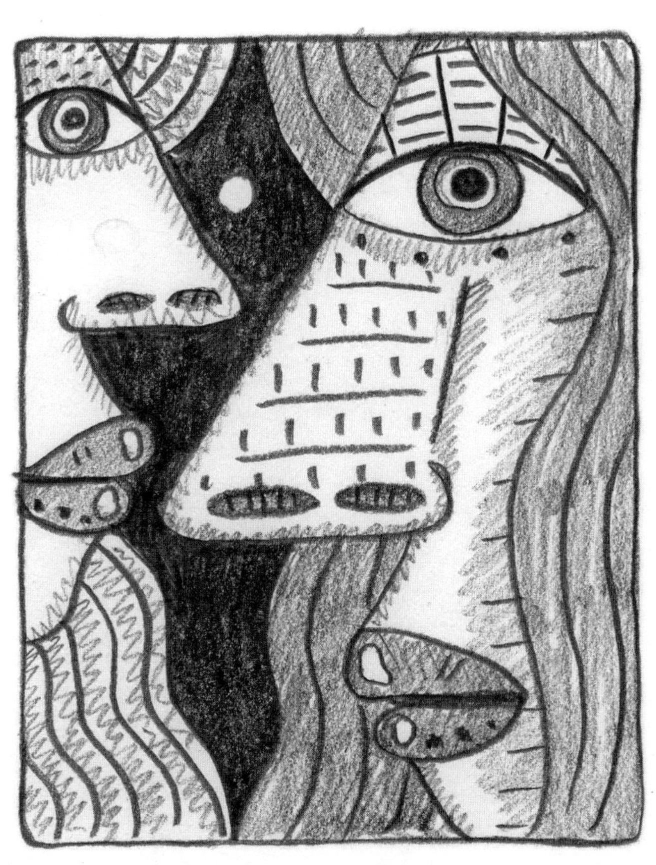

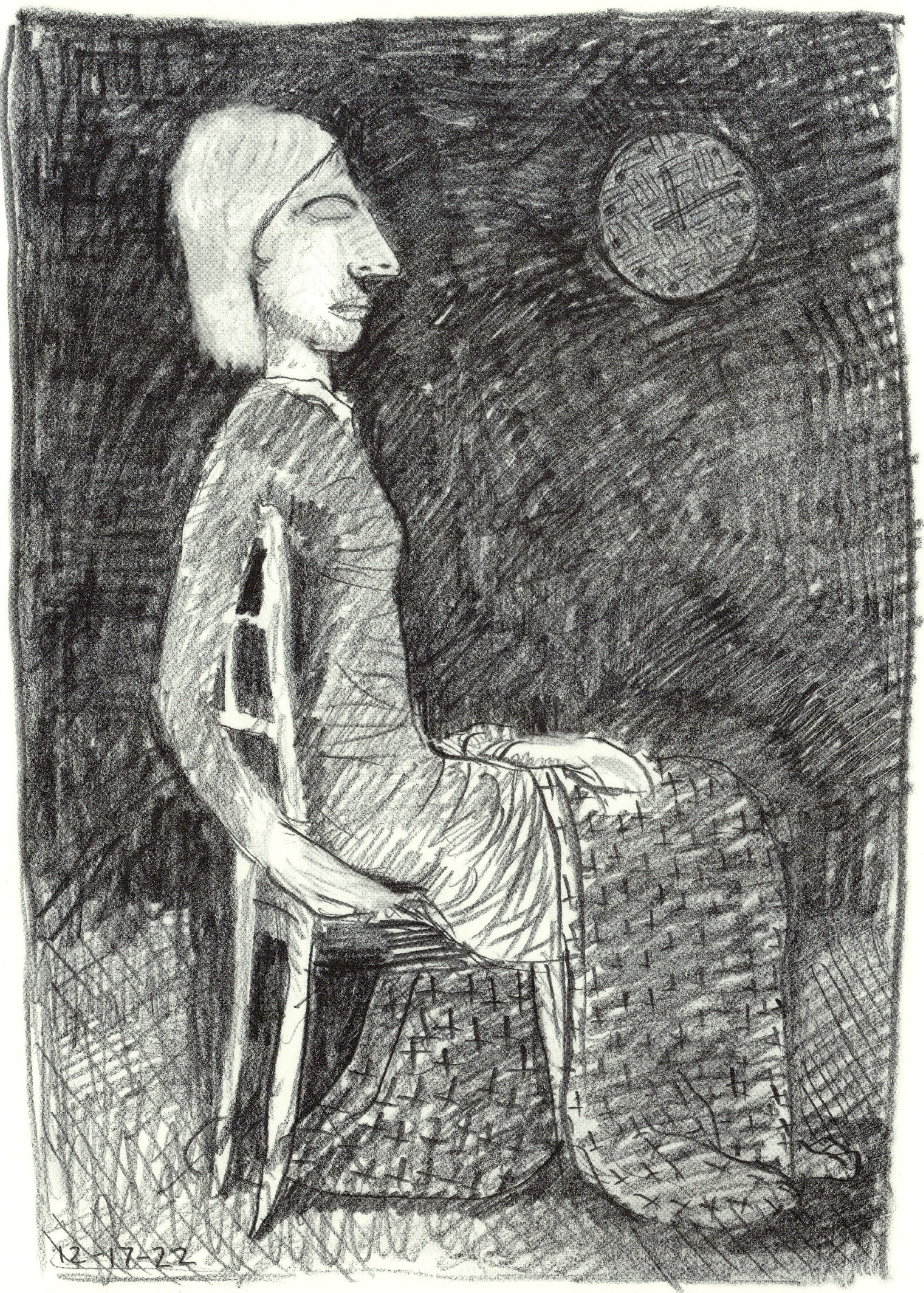
12-17-22

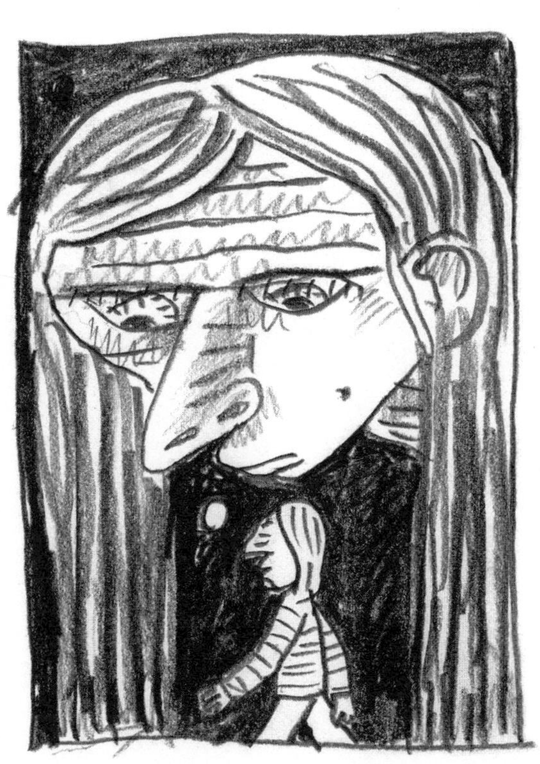

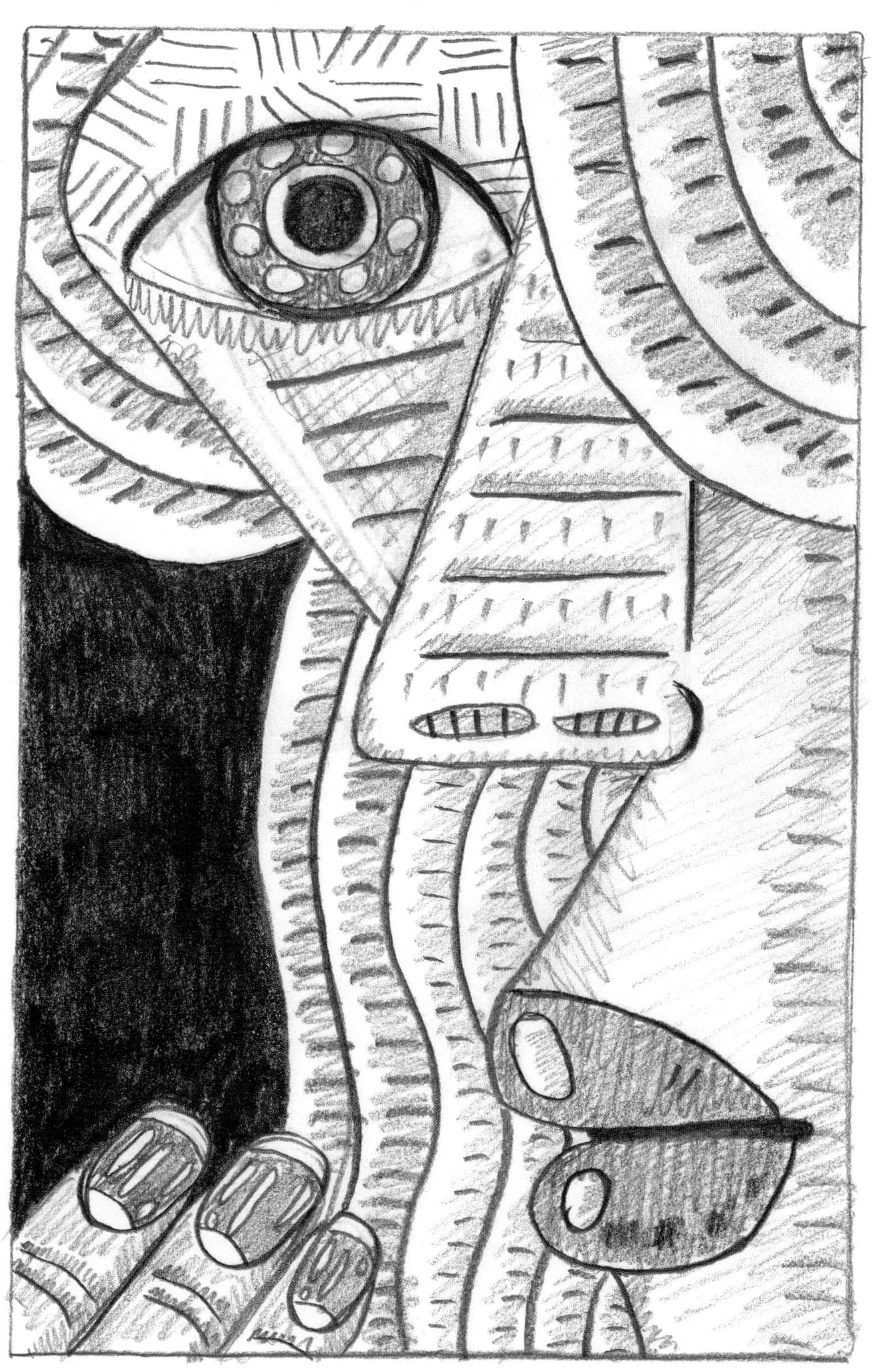

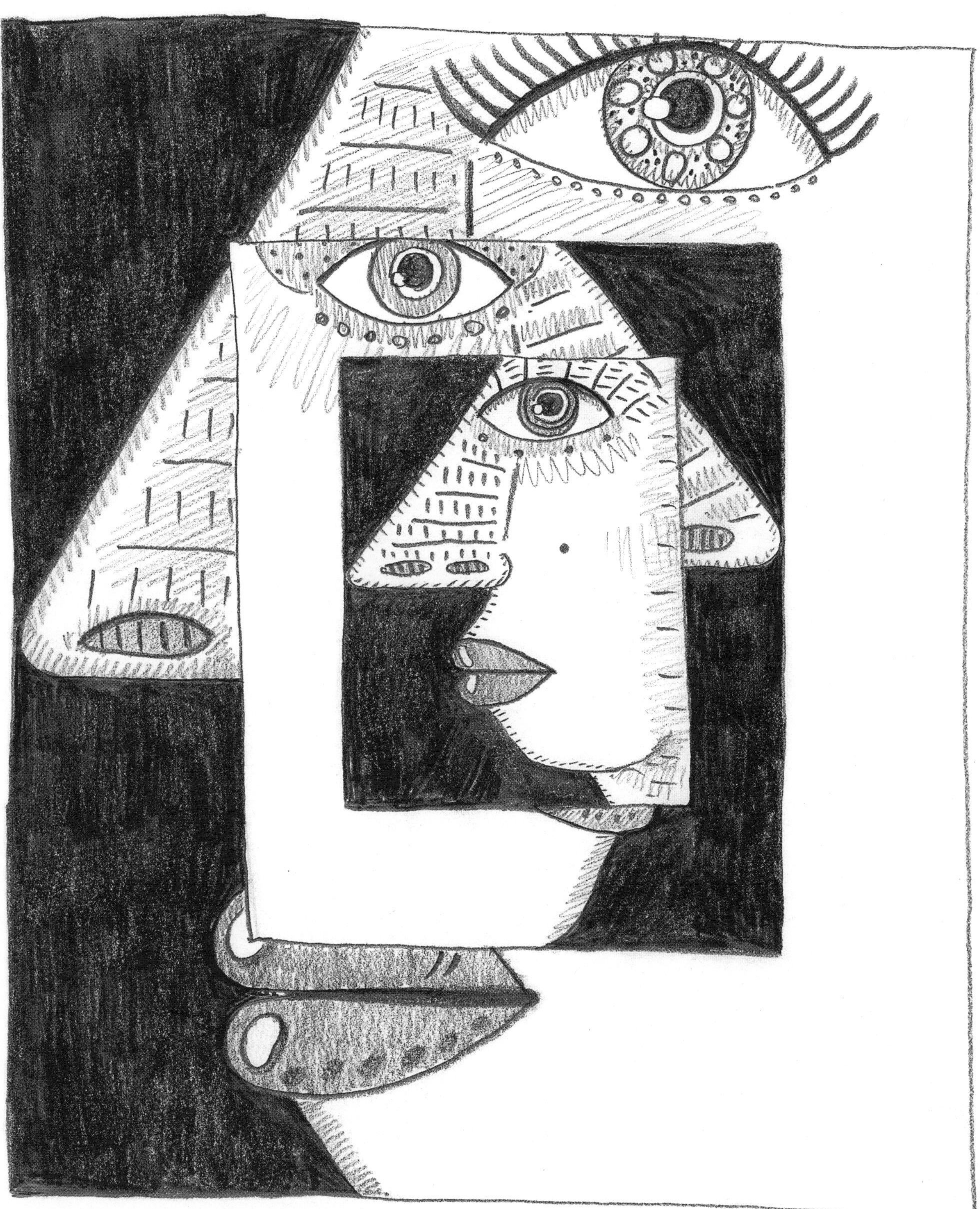

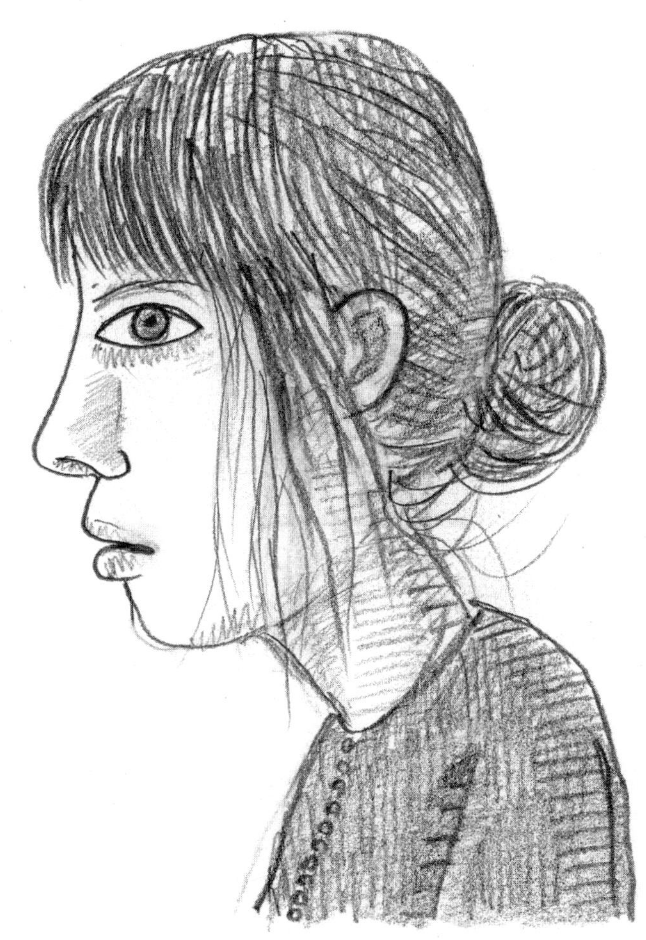

COPYRIGHT © 2024 BY BRIAN CALVIN

ALL RIGHTS RESERVED

PUBLISHED BY FLOOD EDITIONS

WWW.FLOODEDITIONS.COM

ISBN 979-8-9857874-4-3

DESIGNED BY CRISIS

PRINTED ON ACID-FREE, RECYCLED PAPER IN CANADA

THIS BOOK WAS MADE POSSIBLE THROUGH THE GENEROUS SUPPORT OF
THE CHAUNCEY AND MARION D. MCCORMICK FAMILY FOUNDATION.

FIRST EDITION

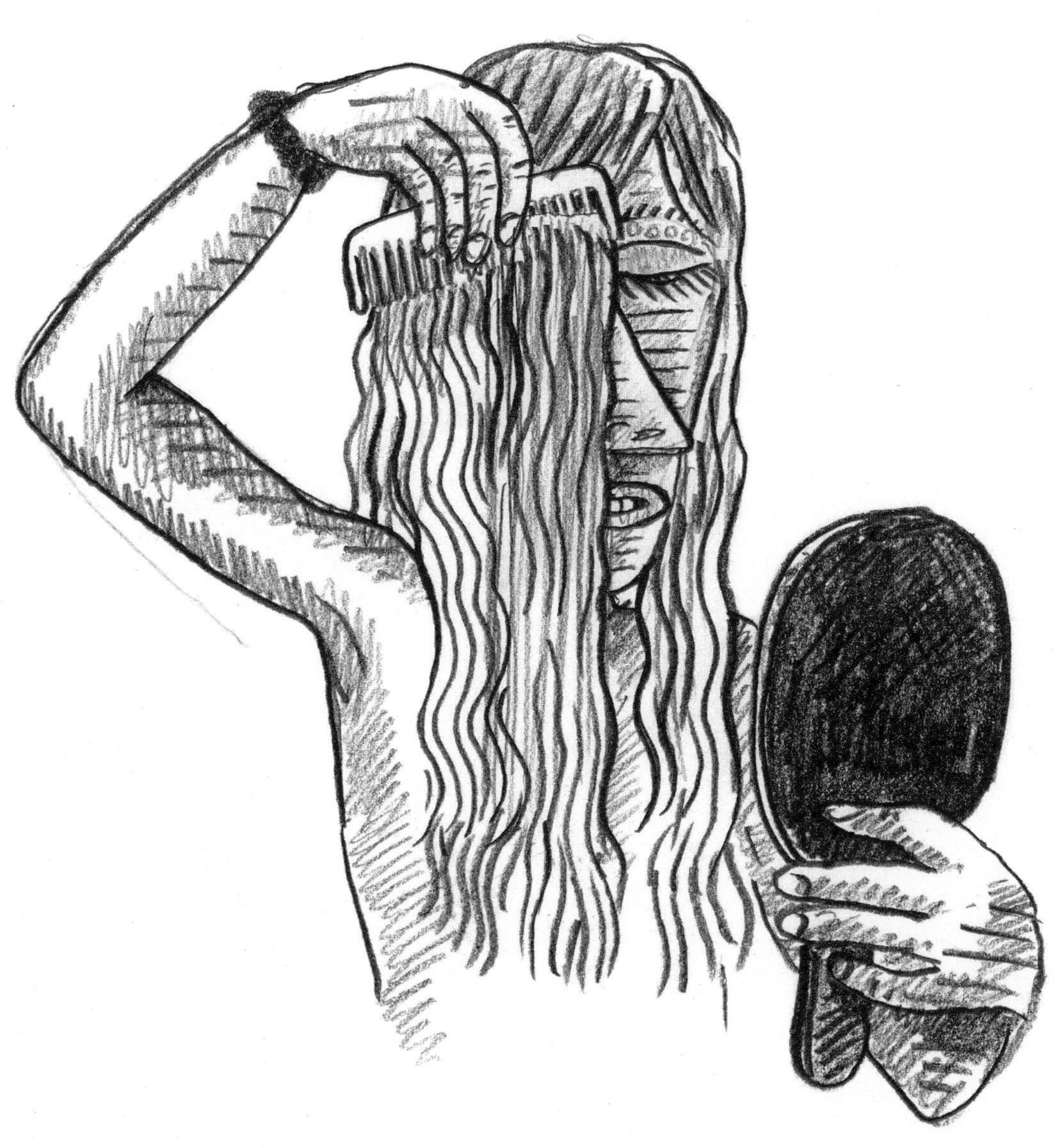